"Time always seems scarce. Money, capacity, labor—these things can be stretched. But not time. Its very march can cramp us and leave us desperate. David Henderson knows all this—and offers a profound reminder of living out of the abundance of God's life and eternity. God's gift of tranquility does not stretch time but makes our time enough. I need—we need—this deep wisdom!"

—**Mark Labberton**, president of Fuller Theological Seminary

"I honestly can't think of a more difficult topic to write about than time. Time itself is given to us as a gift, but we find it a threat. We relish time if it opens up for us and despise it when it is limited. David Henderson is a wise sage, guiding us gently against the fierce tides within our hearts which war with time. David invites us out of our attempts to master time and into the gorgeous spaciousness of entering time in order to listen to God's heartbeat. If you desire more pleasure in life, then you'll be glad you read this book. Yes, this book is worth your time."

—**Janice Meyers Proett**, coauthor of *The Allure of Hope* and national conference speaker

"If you don't have time to read this book, I am sorry for you. And I would advise: take time! David Henderson writes with profound insights and practical directions about redeeming time. As he points out, the deeper concern 'must not be how we manage our time in a busy world but how we manage our inner world in a busy time.' This is thoughtful, practical, wise. Take time to read it. You may find the time of your life."

—**Leighton Ford**, president of Leighton Ford Ministries

TRANQUILITY

TRANQUILITY

CULTIVATING A QUIET SOUL IN A BUSY WORLD

DAVID W. HENDERSON

BakerBooks
a division of Baker Publishing Group
www.BakerBooks.com

Published by Baker Books
a division of Baker Publishing Group
P.O. Box 6287, Grand Rapids, MI 49516-6287
www.bakerbooks.com

Printed in the United States of America

Library of Congress Cataloging-in-Publication Data
Henderson, David W., 1959–
    Tranquility : cultivating a quiet soul in a busy world / David W. Henderson.
        pages cm
    Includes bibliographical references.
    ISBN 978-0-8010-0321-9 (pbk.)
    1. Peace—Religious aspects—Christianity. 2. Quietude. 3. Time—Religious aspects—Christianity. I. Title.
    BV4647.P35H46 2015
    248.4—dc23   2015012095

15 16 17 18 19 20 21   7 6 5 4 3 2 1

To my beloved Sharon Joy with deepest gratitude to God for the inexpressible gift of spending time and sharing life with you. How much richer the journey for your presence in it.
I love you so.

Better one handful with tranquility
than two handfuls with toil and chasing after the wind.

Ecclesiastes 4:6

Contents

Contents

Preface

Do you not rush through the world too hard, Mr. Henderson?

Saul Bellow, *Henderson the Rain King*

Surely if there is anything with which we should not mix up our vanity and self-consequence, it is with Time, the most independent of all things.

William Hazlitt, "On a Sun-dial"

And what, in God's name, is all this pother about?

Robert Louis Stevenson, *An Apology for Idlers*

I wasted time, and now doth time waste me.

William Shakespeare, *Richard II*

Time is a storm in which we are all lost.

William Carlos Williams,
preface to *Selected Essays*

About fifteen years ago, I was asked by a publisher to write a book about time, busyness, and hurry. I was too busy. I suggested we talk later.

A year or so passed, and I was ready—or so I thought. But then God took me from serving as the associate pastor of a church of three hundred to serving as the senior pastor of a church several times that size.

The deadline for the book came and went. I was just too busy. My publisher extended the deadline, and I tried again. Still too busy.

A dozen more years of starting and stopping went by.

At first, it was funny. "Get this! I'm writing a book about busyness, but I'm too busy to write it!" Then it became sad. Then exasperating. At times, it was embarrassing. Several times I came close to giving up.

When I finally finished the book—years after that first contact—the old editor was long gone and the new editor, while gracious, was no longer interested. That God brought Baker Books along at that juncture, and moved them to see something of value in the pages that follow, is tribute to his tenacity, not mine.

As I look back, God has shown me his broader purposes in all of this deferring and delaying. It turns out that when it comes to time, as with all else, God knows just what he is doing. Ten or fifteen years ago, had I managed to finish it, I would have written a very different book, a much tidier book, the sort that comes from merely sticking one's toes into a subject. It would not have been much worth reading.

During the intervening years, God led me farther from the relative safety of the shoreline into the deeper, choppier waters. There, for over a decade, I have been trying to negotiate the more temperamental currents of time, sometimes treading water, sometimes fighting the riptides, often sputtering. And I've become convinced of two things. One, Scripture has more to say about this theme than we think it does. And two, our dealings with time lie much nearer the core of Christian discipleship than we typically think.

In fact, time occupies a unique place in the mind and purposes of God. He uses it to break us and to bless us, to weary us and to bring us rest, to expose our need and his sufficiency, to thwart our ends and accomplish his—all to carry us, in the end, to him.

If it is true, as Thomas à Kempis writes, that God directs all things that direct us to him,[1] then surely time is one of his greatest agents and our frustration with time one of his greatest gifts.

———

Thanks are due in myriad directions.

Rebekah Guzman, my acquisitions editor at Baker, together with my wonderful team in Grand Rapids—Lauren Carlson, Heather Brewer, Mark Rice, James Korsmo: for your valuable contributions to this book and your hopeful sense of its promise.

Sue Kline, my manuscript editor: for the joy of collaborating anew and for your amazing Michelangeline ability to make more of a work by making less of it.

The elders of Covenant Church: for pressing me to see writing as part of my calling and graciously freeing a portion of my time to fulfill that call.

Andrew Patton, Jan Schirack, Radonna Fiorini, and the rest of the Covenant staff: for your support and encouragement. I love being a fellow worker in the kingdom with you.

Covenant Church, as well as my brothers and sisters in the church of Romania, with whom I have been privileged to share some of these insights: for teaching me so much of what it means to love, serve, and follow Jesus.

Tom and Beth Bridge: for sharing a sweet haven for rest, reflection, and writing.

Paul Gould: for your careful reading of several sections of this book as well as your valued friendship.

Dick and Sibyl Towner: for your insights and perspectives and for the eagerness with which you encouraged me to share these thoughts with others.

Scott Freeman and your team at the IARTCC: I'm so impressed by what you guys do!

My Covenant Group: for the ways your lives have compassed mine—in both senses of the word—for nigh on thirty years.

The Mead Men (or the Wrinklings, as I prefer to call you)—Lon Allison, Jerry Root, Rick Richardson, Walter Hansen, and our dear late brother Chris Mitchell: for freely widening your writing group to include me and for your welcome advice and gracious words.

Paul Tripp: for your timely insights all those years ago and for your example as a faithful steward of God-given ideas and insights.

Jim Martin and John VonErdmannsdorff at Von's Booksellers in West Lafayette, Indiana: for the best new arrivals section anywhere. Your exceptional work as an independent bookseller has enriched this book in ways beyond your knowing.

My beautiful wife, Sharon, and my precious children, Brandon (and Christy), Sean, Molly, and Corrie: for the gift of sharing life with you and for your exuberant and unflagging encouragement.

And supremely to God on high, my life, from whom and through whom and to whom are all things—to him be all glory. "If thou dost give me honour, men shall see, the honour doth belong to Thee."[2]

⁓

Now come with me, my fellow time traveler. It's time we jumped in.

Introduction

The River People

Time is a kind of river, an irresistible flood sweeping up men and events and carrying them headlong, one after the other, to the great sea of being.

Marcus Aurelius, *The Emperor's Handbook*

The river of temporal things hurries one along: but like a tree sprung up beside the river is our Lord Jesus Christ. He assumed flesh, died, rose again, ascended into heaven. It was His will to plant Himself, in a manner, beside the river of the things of time. Are you rushing down the stream to the headlong deep? Hold fast the tree. He became temporal that thou mightest become eternal.

Augustine, homily 2 on the First Epistle of John

We are a river people, we human beings, and time is the current in which we live.

From the instant we splash into time, we are swept along by its coursings. We live by it and with it and on it and in it.

1

We are aware of time from the moment the alarm clock jars us from a too-short sleep to the moment we drop back into bed weary and spent at the end of a too-long day. We feel it in the rhythm of the day's routines: showering, shaving, commuting, carpooling, schooling, working, eating, sleeping. We're aware of it in life's patterned requirements: paying the bills, keeping up with the laundry, stocking the fridge, returning phone calls. And we are confronted with it in the moment's pressing demands: when the transmission locks up, the computer goes down, the meeting goes long, the supplies come up short.

We are mindful of time's tenacious, riptide pull. "I've got an appointment across town in ten minutes!" "Somebody needs to get Corrie to her dentist's appointment at eleven!" "Company is going to be here in forty-five minutes, and we still need to pick up!" "This paper is due tomorrow!" In the rapids, the current consumes us, spinning and shoving us about, insisting on the whole of our attention.

At moments, however, our sense of time's ubiquitous presence recedes. Time's cues are hushed. The splash of beepers and chimes, the ripples of demands and commitments fall out of earshot.

We get so absorbed in cleaning out the garage, for instance, or reading a book that we drift like sleepy rafters across the calm stretches of a river. Time's surface is so still and smooth that we are unmindful of the insistent current that yet presses forward beneath us, carrying us along. When we finally extract ourselves from whatever has absorbed us, we are amazed at how time has flown.

Time may seem to stop, but it never really does. Never are we truly still; always are we carried downstream. We can only forget, never escape, time's current.

Reflecting on our elastic experience of time's passing—now rushing, now still—I wrote a poem to capture this:

Time the tumble jumble current in which
we splashed and splattered bob
upswept and thrust along
until of a sudden
it stops

stands

   still

          . . . a
       lazy universe of time
     into one unending moment
        pressed . . .

                when

                   then

                     suddenly
              out of eddied stillness

        we are plucked and tucked
      headlong into the muddy scudding
    swiftly drifting rush of gushing stream.

This book is not about mastering time. It isn't a technical manual like *The Annapolis Book of Seamanship*. It's more akin to Matthew Maury's classic *The Physical Geography of the Sea*. It's designed to help us *understand* time, not merely sail through it.

Instead of asking, "How do we manage *time*?" this book asks, "How do we manage *ourselves* as people who are ever in time's flow?" It is about perspective and focus, yieldedness and willingness, quiet and silence, putting first the things that should be first, waiting and trusting and resting.

In the New Testament, as we'll explore later in the book, we find two words for time:

chronos n. (Gk.): the length of time; time parceled out in equal, undifferentiated bits: seconds, minutes, hours, days, weeks, months, years

kairos n. (Gk.): the width and depth of time; time thick with the presence and purposes of God

Do you remember those exasperating little handheld, sliding-block puzzles? Small square pieces on the game board fill every space but one. The goal of the game is to slide a square into the open space, creating a new space into which you can move another square, which opens up another spot into which you can move yet another square, and so on, until you rearrange all the pieces into a certain pattern. That is a picture of managing *chronos* time: unceasingly shuffling around bits of time in search of the optimal arrangement. Our culture is obsessed with managing *chronos*.

But we're going to focus on *kairos* time. *Kairos* is the spiritual structure to time that lies beneath the surface of its hours and days. It is time laden with the holy purposes of God, time as a gift to be received, not a puzzle to be solved.

―

Often the passing of time feels like a curse. Too fast! Too soon! Too quick! Too late! The ticking of the clock rings in our ears as an accusation, and our daily planner stands as smug witness to our failings. Time taunts us.

We don't often reflect on all that would be absent from our world had God not created time along with matter and space. But think for a moment what life would hold for us were God to pluck us from the river of time and set us down in the changeless constancy of timelessness. No time would mean all is now as it will always be: no old, no new, no past, no future, no maybe, no one day, no once upon a time.

How would we grow if circumstances never changed? How could we make progress if we were not in motion? If time were gone, so would be opportunity, creativity, hope, healing, maturity, forgiveness, growth. Gone too would be leaving and arriving, discovering and learning, moving and improving, deciding and acting.

Could we be human without time?

How does God view time, and how does he wish us to see it? And once we see it his way, how does he want us to live bountifully within its banks and currents? Those are the essential questions with which this book wrestles, for if life within time is God's purpose for us, then what life within time doesn't have is not worth having. And what it *does* have is worth discovering and embracing.

Prologue

The Busy Young Ruler

As Jesus started on his way, a man ran up to him (for the man was late for his next appointment). "Good teacher," he asked, with a glance at his watch, "what must I do to inherit life without end?"

"Why do you call me good?" Jesus answered. "No one is good except—"

At that, the man's cell phone rang. "Hello? Hey, Sam. Listen, I'm, uh, right in the middle of something. Sort of a time-management thing. You gonna be at this number for a while? Great. I'll call you right back."

Jesus waited patiently until the man finished the call. Then he said, "You know the commandments: 'Do not murder, do not commit adultery, do not steal, do not give false testimony, do not defraud, honor your father and mother.'"

The young man had flipped open his planner and started scribbling. Halfway through the list, he stopped writing and looked up, puzzled. He said, "Teacher, those things have been on my quadrant two list since I got my first day planner. I mean, I've been doing this stuff since I was a kid. What else do I need to do?"

Then the man's phone rang again. The man reached for his pocket and turned off the ringer, glancing at the number as he did so.

Jesus looked at him and loved him.

"One thing you lack," he said. "Go clear your schedule of all your self-important activity. Then come and give your time to me. Let me order your days, fill your life with what really matters."

At this the man's face fell. He glanced again at his watch, closed up his planner, and shook his head. He had really hoped for some help. But this?

He gave Jesus's hand a quick shake and said, "Hey, maybe we can do lunch some time." Then he hurried away, for he had a great many things to do, and places to go, and people to see.

Jesus looked around and said, "How hard it is for the busy to enter the kingdom of God!"

The disciples were jolted by his words. But Jesus said again, "Children, how hard it is to enter the kingdom of God. It is easier for a camel to go through the eye of a needle than for a busy man to enter the kingdom of God."

The disciples were even more shocked and said to one another, "What about the whole Protestant work ethic thing? Who then can be saved?"

Jesus looked at them and said, "With man this is impossible, but not with God; all things are possible with God."

Peter said to him, "We have given our every waking moment to you!"

Jesus smiled and put his arm around Peter's shoulder. "I tell you the truth," he replied, "no one who has sacrificed to make time for me and the gospel will fail to receive a hundred times more in this present age—and, in the age to come, time without end. For many who are busy now will have more than enough time on their hands in the day to come. For what is there to do in hell but while away the endless time? But those who carve out time for me now will have purpose and peace for all eternity."

Adapted from Mark 10:17–31

Two Handfuls with Toil and Chasing after the Wind

1

Busy, Busy, Busy

I donna suppose you could aspeed theens up?

Inigo Montoya in The Princess Bride

It takes all the running you can do to keep in the same place.

Lewis Carroll, Alice in Wonderland

God put me on earth to accomplish a certain number of things.
Right now I'm so far behind I think I'll never die.

refrigerator magnet

It is not enough to be industrious; so are the ants. The question
is: what are we industrious about?

Henry David Thoreau, letter to H. G. O. Blake

God, don't let me die. I have so much to do.

last words of Huey Long

All my possessions for a moment of time.

last words of Queen Elizabeth

We sat in a dim room at the Indianapolis Air Route Traffic
Control Center. Eight or nine air traffic controllers, each

with a headset, sat hunched over their twin computer screens. On one was a map tracking a multitude of planes simultaneously, on the other a chart providing readouts on each plane.

Their task was simple enough: get a plane from one side of their airspace to the other. They receive a plane from the air route controller in the adjoining sector, check in with the pilot, track the plane's progress across their territory, radio a farewell, and then hand it on to the next sector. The entire trip across their field takes about eight minutes.

Not so tough, right? But when you add into that same sector another twenty or thirty or forty planes—each at a different altitude, each going a different direction, each climbing or flying level or descending, each on a route that is straight or curved, each going three-fourths the speed of sound—and another half dozen planes coming in or going out of the airspace at any given time, plus the ever-changing factors of airport delays, weather fronts, and planes low on fuel or seeking to make up lost time, the complexity is boggling.

I was observing Scott, a member of my congregation, that day. At the time of my visit, 6,284 commercial flights were in the air above the United States at the same time, crisscrossing from point A to point B. If the average passenger plane holds one hundred passengers, that's more than half a million people—the entire city of Baltimore!—on airplanes over the United States at any given time.

Scott's job as an air traffic controller is the perfect metaphor for the busy life: trying to manage a nonstop, relentless onslaught of things up in the air.

Perpetual Motion Machines

Alicia, a Chicago executive, lives two hours from her corporate headquarters. She sets her alarm for 5:30 every morning and showers and gets ready for her day while her four-year-old son munches a Pop-Tart in front of the TV. Just after seven, she scoops up her son in his pj's and drops him off at her sister's house on her way to catch her train. At the end of the workday, she hops on the train and heads back to the suburbs, arriving home with her son and McDonald's at about 8 p.m. She has barely enough energy to take a bath before she falls asleep on the bed, usually while watching TV with her husband and son. Sometimes when the alarm goes off the next morning, their son is still in bed with them.[1]

Fourteen-year-old Jessie from Norwalk, Connecticut, says her mother and father insist she take only the highest honors classes. "I told my teachers I wasn't ready for them, but did they listen? No. I'll be lucky if I get a D in algebra." If she doesn't go to the best college in America, she's convinced her parents will be angry with her for life. And Jessie pushes herself outside of class as well. She plays clarinet in a marching band, practicing three times a week for three hours and performing in competitions every Saturday. "I am so exhausted that I sleep through the alarm every morning. And if I miss the bus, my mother has a total breakdown. I live on aspirin."[2]

Every day for four weeks, Dan, a sales manager, worked from 6 a.m. until 8 p.m., stopping only for a burger at a fast-food joint sometime during the day. Then he ran home for a quick meal with his wife and a glimpse of his newborn daughter before returning to work at 10 p.m. Around 3:30 in the morning, he headed home for a quick "nap," then got up a few hours later to start all over again. On his way to the hospital after his heart attack, Dan's only thought was, "I really don't have time for this."[3]

Our culture breeds unceasing motion. There is always something else to do. We need, we want, we crave more time. As one researcher noticed, we talk about sleep the way hungry people talk about food.[4]

Crazy Busy

A few months ago, I had this conversation with Radonna, my ministry assistant:

Me: "Is today Friday?"

Her: "Yes, unbelievably."

Me: "So, did you tear one of my days out of this week?"

Her: "Yes, it was Tuesday."

Me: "Do you still have it lying around somewhere? I think it could be helpful."

Her: "No, I'm sorry. I recycled it. I try not to hang on to the past."

Another time Radonna glowered at me and said, "Time is possessed! Whole portions of it just disappear!" I grinned, remembering Alfred, Lord Tennyson's definition of time as "a maniac scattering dust."[5]

Think for a moment about the way we greet each other. "How are you?" we ask. Once upon a time, in a simpler world, the person replied, "I am fine, thank you. And you?" Not any longer. Now, "How are you?" is followed by one predictable response—"Busy"—and its many variations:

"Things are nuts."

"I have so much to do."

"I wish I could clone myself."

"I'm running around like a chicken with its head cut off."

"You wouldn't believe how crazy things are."

"I've got so much to do I can hardly think straight."

We can't stop talking about time. It seeps its way into nearly every conversation. According to the editors of the *Concise Oxford*

English Dictionary, time is the most frequently used noun in the English language.[6]

At a staff meeting the other day, one of my colleagues flopped down in his chair, grabbed his forehead, and sighed. "Whew. Every day is a second and every week is an hour!" When I asked one of my son's friends how she was doing, she threw up her hands and groaned. "I feel like a computer with too many apps on!" A member of our congregation, a professor, said, "It feels like I'm on a treadmill and each year somebody pushes the faster button." His wife nodded and said, "That book on margin has been sitting by your bed for a year, and you haven't had time to pick it up."

I love the quirkiness of *New Yorker* cartoonist Bruce Eric Kaplan. In one of his cartoons, a man talking on the phone says, "I don't have time to talk about this now. Can't it wait until we're dead?"[7]

Another *New Yorker* cartoon (their most reprinted ever) shows a man at his desk talking on the phone and flipping through his day planner: "How about never?" he asks. "Is never good for you?" I can identify with that more than I would like to admit.[8]

Busyness—the hurried, harried life—is epidemic. We are busy, busy, busy, ever scurrying through life.

Booked

The self-help stacks at the local bookstore mirror our hurry. There you will find *One Year to a College Degree*, *Thirty Days to a Better Life*, *Seven Days to a Brand New Me*, even *Sixty-Minute Marriage Builder*. Still not quick enough to address your crisis? How about *One-Minute Father*, *Sixty-Second Stress Management*, *The One-Minute Healing Experience*, *One-Minute Therapist*, or *Sixty Seconds to Serenity*?

More than one hundred titles in print use the word *instant*. You'll find everything from *Instant Yiddish* to *Instant Emotional Healing*. Running out of time? Read *Instant Time Management*.

The Christian publishing world is not immune to the bane of time. Among examples are *Sixty Seconds with God*, *Daily Prayers Sixty Seconds Long*, and *Instant Sermons for Busy Pastors*. Yikes.

Are you feeling it yet? The clenched jaw? The jiggling knee? That ache of anxiousness in your chest? I'm sure you are eager to move from tension to tranquility. But we need first to go a little deeper into the roots of our hurry.

As in the complex interplay of colliding air masses that produce tornadoes, many dynamics, both inside of us and around us, contribute to the whirlwind of busyness and activity in which we find ourselves. In the next two chapters, we'll explore some of them.

2

The Busyness Factory

Don't just stand there. Download something.

T-Mobile ad at the Dallas airport

Never clock out.

motto for
Third Shift Ale

The spirit of the time shall teach me speed.

William Shakespeare, *King John*

We create our own frenzy, our own mass convulsions. . . . The frenzy is barely noticeable most of the time. It's simply how we live.

Don DeLillo, *Cosmopolis*

Don't ever get your speedometer confused with your clock, like I did once, because the faster you go the later you think you are.

Jack Handey, *Deep Thoughts*

The clock and Christ are not close friends.

Richard Swenson, *Margin*

I must govern the clock, not be governed by it.

Golda Meir

17

It was ludicrous. We pulled up to the beach at 4:30 in the afternoon, and I said, "OK, kids, we've got twenty minutes."

We were near the end of our family vacation to the Orlando area, and we had promised our kids at least *some* time at the beach. Animal Kingdom had taken up the whole first day and Epcot the next day. Now, on this third day, we had taken our time getting ready, and by the time we had gotten to the Kennedy Space Center for our three-hour tour, it was already past noon.

Plus, we'd promised our kids some unhurried time at the hotel at the end of the day to swim, play shuffleboard, and watch the Olympics. But we couldn't let that go too late because we needed to turn in early so we could enjoy our final Disney day at Magic Kingdom.

That left twenty minutes. If you had been there during those few minutes we had on the beach, this is what you would have heard. "Brandon, I really don't want to hear it. This is the only time we have to be here. OK, everybody come over here. Time for a picture. Stand right over here. That's great. Come on, Brandon, smile, would you, bud? Hey, look, is that a dolphin? And there's another one. OK, five minutes everybody. Corrie, go rinse your hands. Oh, come on, Corrie, don't do a handstand after you've rinsed your hands. Go rinse the sand off again. OK, everybody to the car. Corrie! You just rinsed your hands. Why did you start digging again? Molly, please don't put your feet in the water. We need to dry off our feet and get in the car, girl. Sean, I'm sorry we didn't get a chance to look for shells, but you chose to use your time digging in the sand. All right everybody, here we go."

The Hendersons do Cape Canaveral. Ain't that a pretty picture.

The press toward busyness comes, I think, from two directions: outside of us and inside of us. Our culture celebrates motion and activity; we cannot help but be swept up in its pace. At the same time, something *within* us thrives on freneticism and finds busyness attractive.

In this chapter, we'll look at the external, societal pressures that propel us into action. In the next chapter, we'll look at the internal, personal reasons for our haste and hurry.

Giving Time a Face

A couple of years ago, I stood next to the oldest operating clock in the world. Dated to 1386, the clock in Salisbury Cathedral is little more than a huge frame housing a cluster of large wooden gears that sits at the base of the bell tower. It has no housing and no face; the ringing of bells marks the hours.

Just three days before, I had stood at the corner of Corpus Christi College in Cambridge, where in 2008 the new Corpus Clock was unveiled. Like its six-hundred-year-old predecessor, it too has no hands, but there the similarity ends. Concentric gold circles mark the time: hours in the center, then minutes, then seconds on the outside ring. Small slits in disks mark the passing time by parting and closing in sequence, allowing slivers of light through and giving the impression of time sprinting in circles around the clock's face.

The most striking feature of the Corpus Clock is perched on top of the disks. The Chronophage, the "time eater," is a demonic-looking locust with needle-sharp fangs, wagging tongue, and blinking eyes that hungrily opens its jaws and devours each minute as it rounds the clock.

"It's terrifying. It's meant to be," explains inventor John Taylor. "Basically I view time as not on your side. He'll eat up every minute of your life. Just as soon as one's gone he's salivating for the next."[1]

For us as citizens of the modern Western world, life is tied inexorably to the clock. All of our moments, waking and sleeping alike, are bound to the ticking (or silent hum) of the timekeeper on our wrist, our side table, our mantle, our computer, our phone. But it has not always been so. Clock time is a relatively recent invention. For much of human history, time was tied to life, not life to time. Time unfolded with the unfolding of the day.

The earliest efforts to gauge time, such as in the age of Abraham, were tied to the slow rotation of the earth. The beginning and end of the day, when the sun crested the horizon at dawn (Gen. 19:15) and again at dusk (Gen. 15:12), were the two definitive moments in each twenty-four-hour period. Hence, dawn became the standard time to meet for business or to march on an enemy. Dusk became the hour of reckoning: the moment by which help needed to arrive or all was lost.

The only other marker in the sun's circuit was the halfway point of the day, when the sun was at its highest. In the Bible, this is called heat-of-the-day (Gen. 18:1) or heat-of-the-sun time (Neh. 7:3), a wonderful time to be found under a tree or in the shade of one's tent (Gen. 18:1).[2]

Other times of the day were necessarily more approximate. For the Hebrews, load-on-the-backs-of-beasts-of-burden time (Gen. 19:2; 1 Sam. 17:16) was early in the cool of the morning, when desert dwellers preferred to do their harder work.[3] Women-go-out-to-draw-water time (Gen. 19:1) was the corresponding period late in the day when the sun began to dip toward the horizon, the air began to cool, and preparation for the evening meal began.

Together, these natural turns in the day created five relatively definable segments: early morning, late morning, midday, early afternoon, and late afternoon.

The desire to divide the day into smaller parts gave birth to the first clock: the shadow clock, an early relative of the sundial, the oldest known of which traces back to Egypt around 1500 BC.[4] Isaiah alludes to this new technology eight hundred years or so after its invention (Isa. 38:7–8 NLT). Until this point, Hebrew had no word for "time" in and of itself. But now, with the development of a timekeeper, time began to have its own substance.

Then began the march toward ever-greater precision in time-keeping. In the Old Testament, the five blocks of the day were the shortest common time denominator, and the word *hour* is never used. But by the time we come to the New Testament, the hour dominates as the favorite measure of time.

Gearing Up

As early as the sixth century, monasteries had established seven standardized times for prayer based on Psalm 119:164: "Seven times a day I praise you for your righteous laws."[5] These were the five discernible moments of each day, plus first and last light. It wasn't until the middle of the twelfth century, however, that the first clock began to mark off these hours mechanically. The canonical hours were announced with the striking of a bell (*clocca*, from which we get our word *clock*), beginning with four chimes at matins, down to one at noon, and back to four at compline.[6]

Urged along by shopkeepers and merchants, clocks moved out of the monastery and into the public square around 1330. From town hall towers and church steeples, they sounded out twenty-four equal hours all through the night and day.[7] It was one of the earliest of these hour-keeping clocks that I saw in Salisbury.

Reactions were mixed. One medieval Frenchman praised the clock and its maker: "The clock is, when you think about it, a very beautiful and remarkable instrument, and it's also pleasant and useful, because night and day it tells us the hours. . . . Hence do we hold him for valiant and wise who first invented this device and with his knowledge undertook and made a thing so noble."[8]

Others had less giddy responses. One Welshman complained, "This turbulent clock clacks ridiculous sounds, like a drunken cobbler. . . . The yelping of a dog echoed in a pan! The ceaseless clatter of a cloister! A gloomy mill grinding away the night!"[9]

Since then, innovations have made timekeepers more precise, more ever present, and more demanding.

The advent of spring-driven clocks (the oldest dates from 1430) made it possible to have a mantel clock in every home, even in every room. Soon after, pendant and pocket watches allowed a person to carry the time about and consult it as often as wished (1510 is the year of the first known pocket watch).[10]

The earliest tower clocks merely *sounded* the hours. Faces and hour hands were added by the mid-1300s. In the 1660s came the addition of the minute hand (dividing off more "minute" portions of hours). This was followed in the early 1700s by the second hand, keeping track of a "second" division of time (mostly as a novelty for use at the race track).[11]

Today, the world standard of time, the NIST-F1 Cesium Foundation Clock—relying on the Cesium 133 atom, which oscillates exactly 9,192,631,770 times per second—is accurate to one second in 316,000 years. More accurate clocks are in the works, such as the hydrogen maser clock, accurate to within one second every 1.7 million years.[12]

The Clock's (Off)Spring

Every technological development has its unintended consequences. The clock is no exception. With the clock came new ways of thinking about how best to live within time—among them the virtues of planning, punctuality, and efficiency.

The Hour Hand

By the mid-1800s, day planners were already common among business and civic leaders. *Planning*, the art of making appointments with ourselves, is a great way to move from intentions to actions. We commit to doing something we value at some other time, freeing us to focus on something else now. I would get little done without this simple tool.

But at what cost do we order our lives by the hour hand? Rhythm and timing are inherent in everything we do from brushing our teeth to having a conversation. When the clock reaches its long arms into our lives and we mark each hour with a new task, the rhythms can quickly become unnatural. We often forget that sixty-minute appointments are rather arbitrarily dictated by nothing but the face of a clock. Why an hour? Why not fifty-three minutes, or seventy-seven?

I find that hour-long appointments are rarely the right amount of time for a pastoral conversation. I either push through to more pressing matters before I've really connected with the person across from me, or I take the time I need for both person and task and then our meeting runs long, cutting into my time with the next person. Now I try to schedule my lunches and meetings so they are truer to the natural rhythm of relationship. I ask myself, *How long might this exchange take if I didn't have a sense of the clock breathing down my neck?* In my experience, that's usually closer to an hour and twenty minutes rather than a precise sixty minutes.

I've also learned to resist the tyranny of the hour hand by allowing some space between appointments. These spaces provide life-giving breaks from the day's demands and allow me to enjoy a chat with another person or a quick stroll in creation to remind myself that God is part of this full life of mine.

The Minute Hand

While mindfulness of the value of time goes back centuries, the virtue of to-the-minute *punctuality* can be traced to the relatively recent past. The late 1800s saw the rise of the world's first assembly lines, with a whole team of workers spread along a conveyor, each performing a single task repeatedly. If just one person is missing, the entire line grinds to a halt. It isn't enough for everyone to be in the right place; everyone must be there at the same *time*.

Ad campaigns in the industrial age began to extol the moral virtue of something called punctuality, and the expression "on time" entered our vocabulary for the first time.[13] Success comes with punctuality; failure is the result of a lazy disregard for the clock. The ad for one company claimed, "If there is one virtue that should be cultivated more than any other by him who would succeed in life, it is punctuality; if there is one error to be avoided, it is being behind time."[14]

Punctuality is crucial for teamwork; it blesses others by showing that we honor their time and value our shared work. When we arrive at an event at an agreed-upon hour, we minimize the time wasted waiting for one another. My staff has patiently challenged me to grow in this area. Immersed in the conversation or project that is before me, I can lose sight of the negative impact on others caused by my lost-in-the-moment enthusiasm.

But taken to an extreme, punctuality insists that clock time always trumps event time. How many activities, conversations, or projects have ended because the clock says it's time, not because the time is right?

The Second Hand

As the industrial complex grew to dominate the economy of the United States in the late 1800s and early 1900s, plant managers were eager to maximize the effectiveness of their workers. Recognizing that profits were directly tied to how quickly their products could be sent out the door, they wrestled to move the line faster and faster.

24

In answer to this demand, a new field of study—"scientific management"—emerged. Experts such as Frederick Taylor and Frank Gilbreth arrived with charts and stopwatches to scrutinize assembly-line operations in what they called time-and-motion studies. First, they broke down every worker's task into its irreducible steps: the forty-two steps required to dig a ditch, for instance, or the eighty-one steps for fastening a flywheel onto a sewing machine. Each of these was then isolated and studied. What was the shortest amount of time in which each individual move of the hand or strike of the hammer could be done? Next, these individual steps were rejoined in what was determined to be the most efficient manner, eliminating wasted motion and shortening task time. Workers were then made to stand in different places, to arrange their tools in different ways, and to carry out their jobs in different sequences to maximize productivity and efficiency and to minimize lost time. Every second counted.[15]

Increasingly, Western culture has been shaped by a concern to see a *return* on our use of time. It isn't enough to be effective, doing something well; now one needs to be efficient, getting more done in less time.

On my way to a gathering in South Africa, I had a five-hour layover in London. Eager not to miss a moment, I took the Tube into the city. On the way back to the airport, I texted my wife: "Hi Honey! Great day in London. Took the Tube in, rode a double-decker bus, St. Paul's Cathedral, art gallery, fish and chips in a park, oldest bookstore in the city—all in five hours. Love you! Your Davey." When I recounted my trip to Griffin, a delightful Welshman at the conference, telling him I "did" St. Paul's and Westminster and the National Gallery, among other things, he grinned and said, "Only an American would speak of *doing* St. Paul's." I could hardly wait to tell him how I "did" Ireland in two days.

If you were to create two columns on a blank piece of paper—one productive time, the other wasted time—and then place in one or the other everything you do, many elements necessary for a vibrant Christian life would fall on the side of waste. Have you ever tried to have an "efficient" relationship? A "productive" time of prayer? An "effective" time of worship? A "fruitful" Sabbath rest? An "industrious" time in creation? An "accomplishment-filled" time of sleep? How quickly things get sideways when we must always have something to show for them.

Planned to the hour, punctual to the minute, productive every second, life has become indistinguishable from industry. The "hard virtues" of planning, punctuality, and efficiency have drained the important but soft dimensions of life—leisure, hospitality, friend-ships, quiet, creativity, art, play, reflection, reading, rest, time in cre-ation—of their legitimacy. These less quantifiable dimensions—the very dimensions that add color and flavor and fullness to life—have become suspect. Not measurable, not quantifiable, they are dis-missed as a distraction from real life rather than seen as a part of life.

Let me conclude this chapter by exploring just one of the many realms of daily life affected by our sprinting, clock-driven culture.

Irkload

Work is the single biggest time consumer for most of us. When we add in getting ready for work and commuting to work, our jobs lay claim to nearly three-quarters of our waking time.

Work's weight is felt in the way we order our calendars. Whereas once the week began on Sunday, with worship as the opening act of the week, now the week is divided between the workweek and the weekend. Sunday has been displaced by Monday as the start of the week, as the layout of many planning calendars reflects.

But work's weight is felt more deeply still.

In many marketplaces, time is a symbol of commitment. James Gleick, in *Faster*, writes, "Managers reward not just the actual work product but the lights still on at night and the steaming coffee cup already visible on the desk at daybreak."[16] Our culture values the sheer quantity of hours spent at work.

I spoke recently with a friend who is on Purdue's faculty. She described the unreal pressures placed on her as a pre-tenured professor. Of course, she needs to teach classes effectively—preparing lectures, grading papers and tests, working with her students—and serve on faculty committees. But then there's raising money. One professor told me of a chart in the department head's office showing how much each faculty member has raised in grant money. Professors are regularly compared to see who is lagging behind in bringing money into the department.

But above all these demands, she is expected to be "productive," by which is meant doing original research in her field and publishing her findings—and in the most respected journals. "We just want you to become the world's leading expert in this area," I said, jokingly imitating what her department head might say. She looked at me wide-eyed. "That's exactly what they told me! Seriously!" If she fails to produce, she will fail to make tenure and will be released to seek other employment. Meanwhile, another eager new faculty member bent on attaining tenure will slide his head into her old yoke and begin to slave away. "Go up or go on" is how another tenure-track teacher put it. "You always have to prove yourself. You can never let up."

A former dean of the Krannert School of Management at Purdue told me of a Michigan businessman who spoke to the students. The man was a nationally recognized entrepreneur with a reputation for doing whatever it takes, often spending the night on the couch in his office to stay on task longer. A student asked, "How did you do it all and still take care of your family?"

Tears came to the man's eyes. He said, "I tell you—I mortgaged my house, I mortgaged my family, and I mortgaged my wife, all for the sake of my work. And the only one I've managed to keep is my house."[17]

As a culture, we confer on the workplace an authority (literally: "the right to be the author") that we don't give to any other influence in our lives—not to our family, not to our church family, not even to God. If the boss says do it, we do it, whether that means coming in early or staying late or working weekends or rearranging vacations or moving to a new location. We respond with automatic and unquestioning obedience, behind which lies, I believe, a misguided belief that our future well-being is rooted in our future prosperity and that our future prosperity is held in the hands of our boss rather than in the hands of God.

Lord of the Clock

Walter Hooper, the gentle-spirited man who served as secretary to C. S. Lewis during the final months of the author's life, recalls meeting J. R. R. Tolkien for the first time. Tolkien gruffly seated Hooper in front of an alarm clock and said, "You've got half an hour." Abashed, Hooper jumped to the purpose of his visit. The moment the clock went off, Hooper rose to leave. At that point, Tolkien, who had been thoroughly enjoying the conversation, stood, pushed Hooper back in his seat, and said, "Stay put! I'm the lord of that clock. *I'll* tell you when you can leave."[18]

Tolkien understood what so many of us have missed. The clock is a wonderful servant but a tyrannical master. It has insinuated itself into every corner of our culture, prodding us into ever-busier busyness. But it finds a responsive echo within; there's something inside us that *needs* to be busy. To that we turn next.

3

The Inner Hurricane

People never feel more alive than when they are busy.

Friedrich Nietzsche

I am this kind of guy, rest is painful to me, and I have to have motion.

Saul Bellow, *Henderson the Rain King*

In our production-oriented society, being busy, having an occupation, has become one of the main ways, if not the main way, of identifying ourselves.

Henri Nouwen, *Making All Things New*

I have the impression that if he didn't complicate his life so needlessly, he would die of boredom.

Boris Pasternak, *Doctor Zhivago*

Busyness is our art form, our civic ritual, our way of being us.

Adam Gopnik, *The New Yorker*

All men should strive to learn before they die what they are running from, and to, and why.

James Thurber, "The Shore and the Sea"

Among the social activities I looked forward to most during my sophomore year at Miami University were the Reid Hall guys' get-togethers with the women from Symmes Hall next door.

On one of those evenings, I sauntered into the room of a lively, curly-haired freshman named Fran and tried to strike up a conversation. I turned to my favorite subject—me—and began enumerating all the things I was involved in. Fran was utterly unimpressed. She looked at me and said, graciously but directly, "David, what are you running from?"

I stammered some sort of answer and stumbled into the corridor. Fran was right. During those years when I was an atheist, I was trying to stuff an empty life with activity, with about as much success as if I were trying to fill an inflatable pool with a hole in it. No matter how much I put in, it would never get full.

A gifted and driven woman recently described to me the near terror she feels at stopping, setting things aside, being unproductive. With tears welling up, she told me that, when she was a child, her mother told her, "Just you wait, little missy. One of these days people will find out what you are like, and you'll be sorry." Her life since has been a whirlwind of unending activity, piling up accomplishments calculated to prove her mother wrong.

Our culture conspires from outside of us, as we saw in the last chapter, to co-opt our minutes and press us into a frenzied rush. But we are more than willing to cooperate, because something within us desires, even *needs*, to be busy.

When people ask us how we are and we tell them we are busy, we don't always say it with remorse. Beneath our whining and complaining may lie pride—or insecurity. The number of appointments on our calendars suggests we are important. We are convinced that the opposite of an empty life is a full schedule, that meaning is found in activity.

Type A Society

Half a century ago, an upholsterer from San Francisco made a curious discovery. He was called to a cardiologist's office to reupholster some chairs in the waiting room. When he looked at the furniture, he wondered immediately what was wrong with the patients. Only the front edge of the seats and the first few inches of the armrests were worn out. "People don't wear out chairs this way," he said.[1]

Five years later, in 1959, Drs. Meyer Friedman and Ray Rosenman began to put the pieces together. They had noticed an odd pattern shared by many of their cardiac patients, a pattern that centered on a "chronic sense of time urgency."[2] Patients showed irritability at being made to wait in line, had difficulty relaxing, and were anxious over delays. Obsessed with not wasting a moment, they spoke quickly, interrupted often, hurried those around them, and were forever rushing. Hence the waiting-room chairs: the patients sat on the edge of their seats, nervously fidgeting at the arms of the chairs as they watched time tick by.

The cardiologists called the new disease "hurry sickness."

According to Friedman, hurry sickness "arises from an insatiable desire to accomplish too much or take part in too many events in the amount of time available."[3] The hurry-sick person is unable to acknowledge that he can do only a finite number of things. "As a consequence, he never ceases trying to 'stuff' more and more events in his constantly shrinking reserves of time."[4]

A few years after their discovery, in the early 1960s, Friedman and Rosenman began to refer to the hurry sick using a more neutral term—type A—allowing the diagnosis of a sickness to become a compliment.

One type A client bragged to his doctors that he could watch four TV sets, ride his exercise bike, and pay his bills at the same time. Another installed a hinged board beside his toilet to get paperwork done while sitting there. And one put his food through a blender so he wouldn't have to waste time chewing.[5] "'How can I move faster, and do more and more things in less and less time?' is the question that never ceases to torment him."[6]

In 1959, those behaviors stood out as bizarre. Today, smoothies are readily available. Multitasking of all sorts—including in the bathroom—is the norm. And news and sports programs give us four programs' worth of material at one time: the talking head speaks about one thing, an image over his shoulder addresses something else, and scrolling across two tickers on the bottom of the screen are scores or news highlights. What's the big deal?

Cardiac psychologists Diane Ulmer and Leonard Schwartzburg identify three troubling symptoms of advanced hurry sickness—troubling because of their implications for our society but also because we see them more and more in the people around us and in ourselves:

1. Deterioration of personality, marked particularly by a lack of interest in aspects of life except for those connected with the achievement of goals
2. Racing-mind syndrome, characterized by rapid, shifting thoughts that gradually erode the ability to focus
3. Loss of ability to accumulate pleasant memories, mainly due to either a preoccupation with future events or a rumination about past events, with little attention to the present[7]

To these can be added a short fuse. If hurry is the way we live, impatient is the way we relate. A British survey found that nearly 40 percent of those surveyed had become more impatient in the previous five years.[8] We are willing to stand in line, stay on the phone, and wait for service for fewer minutes than ever before.

I've come to see that my impatience is an expression of my irritation that things aren't going the way *I* think they should go—the way I feel *entitled* for things to go. How dare the world not run on my schedule! The kids horsing around in the tub and pushing back their bedtime, my wife restating a point that I feel sure I got the first time around, Left Lane Louies slowing down my progress on the interstate, inconsiderate walkers doing the same on the bike path, baristas chatting with the customers in front of me—regardless of the cause, I feel annoyed that my forward progress is impeded. Inevitably, slowpokes are made to pay because their lives are not calibrated to the same crazy clip as my own, my annoyance seeping through in thinly veiled curtness.

What lies behind hurry sickness? The conclusion of Friedman and his colleagues is sobering. In his book on stress, *Why Zebras Don't Get Ulcers*, Robert Sapolsky sums up their findings: "The core of the time-pressuredness is rampant insecurity. There's no time to savor anything you've accomplished, let alone enjoy anything that anyone else has done, because you must rush off to prove yourself all over again."[9]

Busy for the Right Reasons

Faithfulness to life's barest responsibilities—eating, sleeping, and caring for oneself; loving one's family, friends, and neighbors; carrying out one's vocational calling; worshiping and serving God—will necessarily make life full.

On top of these are many other right, legitimate, and God-honoring reasons for our lives to become particularly busy at times:

Financial setbacks may require us to take on another job or work more hours.

The arrival of children may claim our every waking hour (and any number of our sleeping ones!).

The needs of loved ones may call us into service.

A painful end to a marriage may require us to be both mom and dad for our kids.

33

Our vocations may necessitate sacrifices at times.
Ministry or community service may ask more of us for a season.

As I write this morning, with Venus overhead in the predawn sky, I look across the ravine to the home of our good friends, where lights are already on. Six months ago, in a tragic accident, their thirtysomething son was paralyzed from the chest down. His life changed on that day. So did theirs. She moved to the city while her son recovered from his accident and began rehab, and she tended to him. All day. Every day. Last month the family brought him home for the next stage of his recovery. Today, the mom's day is utterly dominated by her son's needs. Why is her life full? Love. Love propelled her to lay aside her own needs and to serve him.

In response to an aside in a sermon, in which I suggested that if we're using an alarm clock we may not be living in keeping with God's design for us, a member of our staff graciously reminded me that his alarm clock allows him to serve his wife and his disabled son. Born with Cri-du-chat syndrome, Michael is missing part of a chromosome, leaving him with a number of physical struggles that make getting through each night a challenge. Rob's alarm clock lets him sacrifice sleep to fulfill his calling as a husband and a father, which he does in ways that are beautiful beyond words.

Whether for reasons as grave as these, or for other less costly reasons, we all find ourselves in seasons that require extra from us—for the right reasons.

And for the Wrong Ones

But sometimes, unhealthy inner needs drive us into busyness. I had a poignant conversation with a physician in our congregation who described how out of whack his life had been because of the number of hours he had devoted to his practice. He was often pulled away from family life, and he deeply regretted it. So when his office staff was restructured, he took the opportunity to cut back on his office hours and to reduce his on-call days.

When I asked him why he hadn't done so years earlier, he was honest. "Competition. My partner is competitive and a workaholic, and I got caught up in that. That made it easy for me to try to keep up with his pace and his schedule." He paused. "And identity. My identity was caught up in my work, in my performance as a doctor." Then he leaned forward and grinned. "It is so good now that I'm trying to figure out if I can cut back my hours even more!"

Sifting through right and wrong reasons for our busyness is challenging. Almost always we will find both kinds of motives side by side in the same action:

A young nurse can work extra hours at the hospital because need requires it and, at the same time, because she wants people to think she is heroic in her sacrifices.

A daughter can serve an ailing mother out of love and, at the same time, because her identity has become wrapped up in meeting her needs.

A man can be diligent in carrying out his vocation and, at the same time, can escape from a difficult relationship at home by allowing himself to get caught up in work.

The lures and snares are many. I can be driven to hurry and busyness for many suspect reasons:

I want to impress others.

I lose sight of God's hand in difficult circumstances and fall into believing it is all up to me to bring about a new outcome.

I want to establish my significance in something other than God's love for me.

I wrongly believe that I'm the only one who can meet a particular person's need.

I want the excitement of doing something new or adventurous.

I want to justify to myself that I'm earning my salary.

At root, I recognize that I am most often driven to busyness by believing two persuasive lies: it's all up to me, and it's all about me.

Running in Idol

Busyness is often—not always but often—the means by which we seek to wrest from this world, its residents, and its furnishings that which only God can be for us and do for us.

Isn't that the essence of idolatry? We sophisticated modern Westerners are smugly amused to think of someone being so BC as to fashion a little clay figurine, place it on a stand, and bow down to it. And yet which of us does not have our own altars on which we've placed our career path, or our friends' opinions of us, or our alma mater, or our desire for comfort or fulfillment, or time itself?

You're familiar with the car dashboard lights that flicker on when something is wrong under the hood. In a similar way, warning lights can begin to flash in the human spirit, exposing the idolatry that lies deeper within. Author and counselor Paul Tripp identifies the demand for comfort, respect, appreciation, success, or control as sure signs that God has been displaced by an idol. Other warning signs that things are amiss under the hood may include comparison, competition, or a critical spirit.

Each of these points, in the end, to an inner throne from which God has been displaced and upon which lurks some inferior object of our devotion. Consider three of the many ways our bent, idol-worshiping interiors can inadvertently cooperate with our culture's insistence that we be busy.

Fear of Missing Out

In economics, "opportunity cost" refers to the cost we experience when we forgo one thing for the sake of something else. In a world of instant communication, we are painfully and continually confronted with opportunity costs. Texts, photos, and live streaming hold before us many real-time alternatives to whatever we may be doing in the moment.

As a result, a franticness marks the way many of us make decisions about how best to use our time. If we go to the reunion this weekend, we'll miss the get-together at the lake, the service project at the church, and the game on TV. What to do? If I grab some fast food with these friends, I can't go to the mall with those friends or the movie with those other friends. What now? In the Middle Ages, victims were drawn and quartered. We experience our own version of that today, victims of a world that, moment by moment and day after day, pulls us in countless directions.

Kelley Watson and Diane Wells, close friends as children, found themselves increasingly torn as they grew older and developed other friendships. They wanted to be with others, but they wanted to do things together as well. They were anxious about missing out on a good time with one another, concerned that memories were being made that they would not both be a part of. They wished they could be in two places at the same time. In 1985, they coined an expression to describe their feelings: FOMO—the fear of missing out.[10]

There seems to be only one solution to FOMO. FIAI—fit it all in. Or die trying.

Offspring Deprivation Anxiety

As soon as our children are born, pressure mounts to give them the perfect childhood. I call it offspring deprivation anxiety (ODA). We live in grave fear that we will ruin our children for life if we fail to provide them with the right portfolio of experiences: instrument lessons, art instruction, language studies, extra tutoring, gymnastics classes, sports camps, summer camps, specialty camps, school sports teams, county sports teams, travel sports teams, service projects. We stack each on the next in the hopes of building the perfect résumé for the perfect future. But at what cost to the present? And at what cost to our kids?

Snow forts and creek walks and building-block cities and imaginary friends and under-the-Ping-Pong-table hideaways are exchanged for chord sequences and passing drills and dawn-to-dusk schedules. Childhood—that wonderful, wanderingly endless time when open days breed boredom and boredom breeds creative play and exploration and reflection—is threatened with extinction. Instead, we turn our children into grumpy, overscheduled miniadults and pit them against one another in a Darwinian competition for future opportunity.

I'm not advocating expunging all things organized from our kids' lives. Group activities foster cooperation and patience. Sports teach civility, leadership, and humility. Art and music enrich our souls and foster creative expression. Camps spark growth, develop responsibility, and build friendships.

What I'm challenging is the way of thinking that lies behind our frenetic family lives. Dave Barry captured our parental fears and pressures when he wrote in his humor column about a meeting at his daughter's preschool regarding selecting the right kindergarten. The message that came through was this: "You need to get your child into the right kindergarten program, so that she can get into the right elementary-school program, without which she cannot get into the right middle-school program, without which she can't get into the right high-school program, which means SHE WILL NOT GET INTO HARVARD BECAUSE YOU FLUSHED HER LIFE DOWN THE TOILET BY PICKING THE WRONG KINDERGARTEN WHEN SHE WAS 5 YEARS OLD YOU WORTHLESS UNCARING PARENTAL SCUM."[11]

Offspring deprivation anxiety stems from the belief that our kids' futures are in our hands. Do we really have that kind of control over the future well-being of our children? Is that a faith perspective? Scripture teaches that it is not we but God who orders the affairs of people. Our destinies—and our children's—are in his hands.

Screening Our Time

Fear and insecurity drive us to drive our children. Boredom and discontentment lull us into the consuming spell of entertainment.

Life is challenging enough to wear anyone out. A great movie, football game, or electronic chat with a friend can ease the burden of life's weightier side. Films such as *Les Miserables*, *Saving Grace* (the one about the pope, not about pot), and *Chariots of Fire* are rich with reward. Lighthearted movies such as *The Princess Bride*, which I regularly quote in my sermons, have an important place in bringing refreshment to our souls and laughter to our lips. But there is a line somewhere, on the other side of which entertainment begins to undermine our lives rather than enrich them.

To express it bluntly, when we are under their control rather than they under ours, screens become time-sucking, life-leeching monsters. When we're not at work or asleep, three-fourths of our time goes to screen-based entertainment, whether movies, TV shows, games, social networking, or the internet.[12] The Kaiser Family Foundation reports that the average child between the ages of eight and eighteen spends a whopping four hours and twenty-nine minutes watching TV, another twenty-five minutes watching movies, one hour and twenty-nine minutes on the computer (for entertainment), and another hour and thirteen minutes playing video games *every day*, and often at the same time.[13]

Unchecked entertainment leeches away our time and soaks up our attention, drawing us from the moment at hand. It disrupts our real-time relationships with the virtual urgency of tweets and texts and tumbling images. It pulls our focus off the people around us, the circumstances before us, the God over us. A life of faithfulness to God requires that we give careful thought to the place of entertainment in our lives.

Soul Satisfaction

All of this leads us to the foundational motives that impel our decisions and actions and make it so easy for us to succumb to our culture's pressure to chase busyness.

What are our deepest needs as broken, finite, God-dependent human beings? Inevitably, I return to five questions regarding our identity and significance:

1. Who am I? (understanding what is true about me and what defines me)
2. What is the reason for my being? (having meaning and purpose in life, knowing why I am here)
3. Is what I do important? (appreciating the uniqueness and significance of what I do)
4. Am I worthwhile? (knowing that I have intrinsic worth and value regardless of what I do)
5. Am I loved? (being valued and accepted for who I am, confident that I am both known *and* loved and have a place of belonging in the heart of another)

Like five hungry and unruly children, these five questions follow us into each circumstance and relationship. Scrambling to satisfy the needs these questions represent, we drive ourselves headlong into activity. If I do this, or this, then I will establish who I am; if I do this, or this, then I will justify my being here; if I do this, or this, then people will think well of me; if I do this, or this, then I can think well of myself.

God means for us to have these deepest needs met *in him alone.* He made us for relationship with him, to love and serve and delight in him and to know his love for us. The sort of love relationship for which God made us is possible only through Jesus, his Son. When we open our hearts to him and believe in him, placing the weight of our lives on him, he brings us into restored friendship with the Father and into new and vibrant life in the Spirit. And all of this is through no effort of our own (Eph. 2:8–9).

Listen to how God answers our deepest needs:

1. Who am I?

   I created you uniquely, like no other. You belong to me. You exist for me. Your identity is defined by your relationship with me: I am your Creator and you are my creature, I am your Father and you are my child, I am your Lord and you are my servant, I am your Redeemer and you are my witness, I am your Friend and you are mine (Exod. 28:36–37; Ps. 100:3; Isa. 43:5, 10; Luke 17:7–10; John 1:12–14; 15:13–15; 1 Cor. 8:6).

2. What is the reason for my being?

   To live for me. To honor, please, love, serve, and obey me, the Lord your God, and to love those I place around you, laying down your life for them. Whatever you do, do it all in the name of the Lord Jesus Christ, living your life to the praise of my glorious grace (Deut. 10:12–13; Matt. 22:37–39; Rom. 11:36; 1 Cor. 10:31; 2 Cor. 5:15; Eph. 1:11–12; Col. 3:17; 1 John 3:16).

3. Is what I do important?

   Yes! I have richly gifted and equipped you to make an eternal difference. I have prepared good works for you to do. All you do is rich with value as you do it for me and I do it through you. I have made you capable; your ability comes from me (1 Cor. 3:11–14; 4:7; 12:14–18; 2 Cor. 3:5; Eph. 2:10; 4:16; 2 Thess. 1:12–13).

4. Am I worthwhile?

Yes, you are of great worth and value. I knit you together in your mother's womb. I was so happy when you came into being. There is no one else like you. You were made in a way that inspires awe and praise. You bear my divine image. You are my workmanship, my masterpiece. You drip with manifold gifts and abilities and insights. You tower above all other creatures, and you are crowned with glory and honor (Gen. 1:27, 31; Pss. 8:5; 100:3; 139:13–14; Prov. 8:31; 1 Cor. 12:4–7; Eph. 2:10; Rev. 4:11).

5. Am I loved?

Yes, I rejoice over you! I delight in you! I chose you before the foundation of the world to be the object of my affection. In love, I gave you life; in love, I gave you *my* life. There is nothing you can do to make me love you less—or more. Nothing can separate you from my love. You are precious to me and honored in my sight, and I love you (Ps. 33:5–9; Isa. 43:4; Zeph. 3:17; John 3:16; Rom. 8:38–39; Gal. 3:1–5; Eph. 1:4–8; 2:8–9; 1 John 4:10).

I was fashioned uniquely by God. I exist to please him. Who I am and what I do matter greatly to him, and I am dearly loved. If we were to let these realities sink down to our bones, to shape us and inform us and define us, how different our lives would look. Think of the many misguided and empty efforts to feel valued or important or loved we could lay down.

In Brennan Manning's inviting *Abba's Child*, he quotes from the journal of John Eagan, who wrote, "Define yourself radically as one beloved by God."[14] At the root of who we are, at the core of our being, this is what is true about us. Not what we accomplish, not what we contribute, not what we do to earn the pleasure of others, not how we busy ourselves but how God views us before we lift a finger. What we do does not define us. God does.

The woman who told me of her mother's harsh words wiped the tears from her eyes and smiled tentatively. These truths were sinking into her heart. She told me that she had just laid aside a business that had become mere busyness, and she was beginning, just beginning, to believe she was loved even when she wasn't in motion.

What peace, what rest can be ours when we are anchored to something more substantive than our never-ending effort and activity. I learned this when, two years after my painful conversation with Fran, I gave my life to Christ. Soul filled, finally, I began to lay aside the froth of activity with which I had sought to stuff my empty existence and for the first time allowed God to lead me into the life he had for me.

⌁

I remember a dawn walk in the mountains of North Carolina. As seems so often the case, though my body was there, my mind was elsewhere, cluttered to distraction with thoughts of the many things clamoring to be done.

As I walked down the trail, my mind racing, I came upon a meadow. Trees stretched skyward. Birds trilled. Pink dripped from the sky. I had stepped into the middle of a drama unfolding. Hanging from each blade of grass in that wide field was a glistening drop of dew. There were tens of thousands of them. I was in awe.

I didn't hear a voice, but God spoke: "I've already been hard at work since long before you rose, but you're welcome to join in."

It isn't all about me. And it isn't all up to me. Jesus said, "My Father is always at his work to this day, and I too am working" (John 5:17). Only in this assurance are we able to lay down our idolatrous activity and find soul rest. Our lives may still be full, but we won't be scrambling. Not anymore.

4

Toward a Solution

Only Robinson Crusoe could have everything done by Friday.

Author unknown

I sense there is something wrong with a day whose projected success is predicated on an allowance of 30 seconds per conversation.

Andrée Seu, *World Magazine*

Beware the barrenness of a busy life.

attributed to Socrates

Why did God give us two hands if not to do two things at once?

Ralph Keyes, *Timelock*

If your wakin', eatin', and haulin' in 3 seconds, you're bookin' yourself too tight.

Brian Regan, *Comedy Central Presents*

Koyaanisqatsi: Hopi word meaning "a life that is so crazy that it calls for a new way of living."

Christopher J. Moore, *In Other Words*

Children's author Jan Brett tells the fable of a little boy's mitten dropped in a wintry woods. Seeking shelter from the chill, a rabbit hops over to the mitten and noses its way in. The rabbit is followed by an owl, a badger, a hedgehog, and finally a bear, all squeezing into the wildly stretched mitten in search of protection from the cold. Then a tiny mouse squeezes into the mitten and climbs on top of the bear's nose. The bear sneezes, which bursts the mitten and launches the menagerie back out into the snow.

That mitten is like our lives, into which we try to shove all manner of things for which there is no room. Our efforts promptly land us in the busyness trap.

The busyness trap	Trying to fit an infinite number of activities into a finite amount of time.

This trap fuels our stress and robs our peace, raises our blood pressure and lowers our effectiveness. It is the source of much of our consternation and the bane of a life of tranquility. Now what?

Time Tampering

Hand in hand with the invention of clock time came a parallel invention: time management. Seven hundred years ago, Stephen Covey's predecessors were writing tracts suggesting ways to make better use of time. Among the ancient suggestions can be found some surprisingly modern advice: create schedules, sleep less, and do more than one thing at a time.[1]

I think of time-management techniques as "timehorns." Just as a shoehorn is designed to wedge a foot into a shoe that's snug, these time-management tools are meant to help us squeeze just a bit more into an already full calendar. Some tools are valuable, others are questionable, but all of them prove in the end to be inadequate solutions to the challenge of fitting an infinite number of things into a finite amount of time.

Here is the current arsenal of weapons against time.

Shaping time. This is the domain of to-do lists and day planners. Their goal: to schedule our time for maximal efficiency. We make a list of all we want to accomplish and put the items into priority order. Alongside that list, we lay out all the time available to us using a calendar or planner. We fill in all the spoken-for slots: work, sleep, meals, showering and dressing at the start of the day. Then, in the time that's left, we make appointments with ourselves to get the remaining items done. Starting with the most important, we write down commitments at specific times on the calendar. Let's see, my numismatic meeting goes in this slot, Junior's orthodontics appointment goes here, we can put ballroom dancing lessons here, and this month we can fit church in here.

Shaving time. The goal here is to do what we have to do in less time, shaving off minutes for other important activities. Find the shortest route home. Carry as many things as possible at one time. Arrange the dishes so those we use most are nearest to hand. Combine and map out our errands. Sort our mail by the trash can. Run while we cut the grass. Go through the ten-items-or-less line at the grocery store. Don't fold the clean underwear. Move closer to work. Learn the quickest way to iron a shirt. Use automatic withdrawals to pay the bills.

Shifting time. Time shifters find a more convenient time to run errands or enjoy recreation. Staffed-24/7 driving ranges, hair salons, car washes, workout facilities, pet clinics, child care centers, bank branches—even museum exhibits—will accommodate odd hours.

Streamlining time. Streamlining came in with the rush of the twentieth century, smoothing flat surfaces and rounding sharp corners to allow vehicles—bullet trains, sports cars, fighter planes—to slip through the airstream more quickly. Today, dozens of time-trimming innovations help us streamline our time: electric razors, blow dryers, home exercise equipment, speed dialing functions, riding lawn mowers, no-iron shirts, overnight mail, Velcro, drive-through car washes, garage door openers, premade meals, prefab houses. And the quintessential time-saving device: the microwave.

Sharing time. One of the easiest ways to save time doing things is not to do them at all. We can delegate our responsibilities to someone else. Have our secretary schedule our appointments, have our kids empty the dishwasher, have our spouse return a phone call, have our roommate water the plants.

No one around with a spare minute? We can hire someone. Merry Maids will clean our house while Hire-a-Handyman fixes that broken screen door. Extended Family Foods will cook a week's worth of dinners or breakfasts and deliver them to our door. (Breakfasts come in ready-to-commute paper bags.)

Elephant Secretary remembers important birthdays, anniversaries, and holidays; picks out cards; and sends them to family and friends for us—complete with a note in our handwriting.[2] Lifestyle managers such as Serenity Now and On the Go 4 U will do whatever we can't get around to. Ezra Glass, one such rescue worker, has been paid to walk the dog, wait for the cable guy, pick up kids from school, take cars to be serviced, plan a last-minute vacation, even organize a funeral. "People are ceding more and more of their lives to others," he notes.[3]

Skimping time. This means spending less time on one thing to make time for something else. Don't read the morning paper. Skip breakfast. Skimp on sleep. Make church optional. Shorten our vacation. Drop out of Bible study. Make our meetings shorter. Work on our days off. Neglect one-on-one time with our kids. Scrap date nights with our spouse.

Sadly, skimping time became part of my strategy during a recent three-year-long season of extra demands with a short staff. I threw exercise overboard. I cut way back on time with friends. Two or three times a week, I missed my morning devotional time. I worked on my days off. And, for the first time in my life, I started drinking coffee. Not good. Worse, now that the crunch time is behind me, I'm struggling to get those things back into (or out of) my life.

Stacking time. If we're trimming back as much time as we can from what we're already doing and still running out of time, we can take the next step: double up.

The term *multitasking* was first used by computer scientists in the 1960s to describe a single computer that served multiple users on a network by swiftly shifting back and forth between tasks.[4] It proved to be the perfect term for doubled-up tasks.

Our culture encourages many creative two-tasks-at-a-time combinations. Watch the news while preparing a meal. Learn a language while cutting the grass. Read a magazine while going to the bathroom. Watch a movie while doing homework. Multitasking while driving has become the norm. Sixty percent of fast food is eaten by "dashboard diners," many of whom are talking on cell phones, jotting down notes, checking maps, and listening to music all at the same time.[5] Mea culpa.

Scientists have proven that the human brain can do only one thing at a time. So what we call multitasking is really back-and-forthing, which means not increased but decreased effectiveness. "People performing two demanding tasks simultaneously do neither one as well as they do each one alone," one study found.[6] I learned this in a startling way when, while driving to a meeting, I realized I wasn't sure where my cell phone was. As I drove, I began to search around inside the car, lifting papers off the passenger seat, fishing around on the floor. When I finally found my phone, I burst out laughing. I was talking on it.

But there is a concern deeper than mere ineffectiveness. Multitasking has a high relational cost. Even a glance at our phone conveys that the person in front of us is unimportant and not worth our time, just another of many tasks to be juggled. Linda Stone coined the term *continuous partial attention* to describe that especially insidious version of multitasking in which we try to do two simultaneous tasks that both require our full attention. We attempt both but do neither well. Texting under the table while visiting with friends, emailing while talking on the phone, talking on the phone while watching TV: we think we are so clever, but our friends—well, our friends just think we are rude.[7]

A man applying for a position at our church hopped in my car at the airport. Within ten minutes of getting in the car, as I was answering a question he had asked about the church, he pulled his phone out of his pocket and began to text. He didn't get the job.

The Momentous Exchange

While some of these timehorns are suspect, skimping and stacking in particular, others have an appropriate place for us as followers of Christ. Scripture consistently urges our wise use of time:

> Teach us to use wisely
>   all the time we have. (Ps. 90:12 CEV)

It cautions against wasting time on "worthless pursuits" (Prov. 12:11 ESV). Rather, the Word pleads, "make the best use of your time" (Eph. 5:15 Phillips).

Time-saving techniques acknowledge time as a gift. Our moments are precious and should be well stewarded. But while time-management tools have their benefits, they also have their costs, some grave and far-reaching.

Time fretting and time flitting. Our moments matter—but our culture's concern is for smaller and smaller increments of time. "Take all the swift advantage of the *hours*," William Shakespeare admonished late in the 1500s.[8] A century later, Puritan Richard Baxter urged his congregation, "Do not trifle away a single *minute*."[9] A campus ministry at Purdue recently hosted an event called "Make Every *Second* Count."

The more each minute counts, the greater becomes the pressure to use each minute optimally. Every commitment comes with an opportunity cost, the loss of some other thing we could be doing instead. This can lead to reassessing constantly how we are spending any given moment. "Am I doing the best thing? Should I be doing something else instead?" Moment-by-moment evaluation of how we are spending our time can sometimes cause us to jump fruitlessly from thing to thing.

Yesterday I walked into a jewelry store to pick up a watch that was being cleaned. I had already decided, undecided, and then redecided to include the watch shop on my itinerary of six carefully mapped-out errands in a not-long-enough stretch of time.

One other customer was in the store when I walked in. "I know it's only a quarter-size difference," she was saying, squeezing on a ring, "but if it's too small, it pinches—like this—and . . ." Before she finished her sentence, I was already weighing whether it was worth waiting. If I stayed, how long was she likely to be? I walked to the door. But if I left, when was I likely to be back to this part of town? Would I waste more time by leaving and coming back later or by staying? I walked back toward the counter. I couldn't believe I hadn't brought along a book.

Resisted interruptions. Sometimes our greatest gifts are those God gives us in the form of disruption. An unexpected word of encouragement, an insight, a chance conversation that blossoms into spiritual matters, an idol exposed, a fresh opportunity to trust God with outcomes—God delights to give us gifts through disruptions in our schedule.

A few weeks ago, I stepped into my associate pastor's office just as he was heading off to teach. Did he have a moment for a quick question? "Certainly!" was Rob's immediate reply. I apologized for snagging him just before he was jumping into ministry. "Grateful for the opportunity to trust God and enjoy his provision," was his grinning reply. And he meant it.

Misplaced efficiencies. "Look how much I got done!" we say, holding up our crossed-out to-do lists. Scripture gives us a different measure of accomplishment:

> Make every effort to add to your faith goodness; and to goodness, knowledge; and to knowledge, self-control; and to self-control, perseverance; and to perseverance, godliness; and to godliness, mutual affection; and to mutual affection, love. For if you possess these qualities in increasing measure, *they will keep you from being ineffective and unproductive* in your knowledge of our Lord Jesus Christ. (2 Pet. 1:5–8, italics added)

But we rewrite the text: "Make every effort to add to your work meetings; and to meetings, conference calls; and to conference calls, breakfast appointments; and to breakfast appointments, workouts; and to workouts, lawn work; and to lawn work, home improvement projects. For if you engage in these activities in increasing measure, they will keep you from being ineffective and unproductive."

A concern for efficiency and productivity, for making every minute count, can lead us to view others as resources to be used or as interruptions to be avoided rather than as people to be valued. Just the other day, a member of our support staff admitted that when I passed by her office at seven miles an hour and called out, "How are you?" but didn't slow down to hear her answer, she felt hurt, as though she didn't matter to me. And how would she know otherwise?

A long time ago, I learned not to greet my wife on the phone with "What's up?" Relationally wired as she is, that greeting seems to say, "Enough of the pleasantries. What is the task we need to address so that I can be done with you and get on to other (more important) things?"

In a conversation in her novel *Jane Eyre*, Charlotte Brontë captures powerfully the potential poverty of a life bent upon corralling *chronos*:

Take one day; share it into sections; to each section apportion its task: leave no stray unemployed quarters of an hour, ten minutes, five minutes—include all; do each piece of business in its turn with method, with rigid regularity. The day will close almost before you are aware it has begun; and you are indebted to no one for helping you to get rid of one vacant moment: you have had to seek no one's company, conversation, sympathy, forbearance; you have lived, in short, as an independent being ought to do.[10]

Relationships are inherently inefficient. All involve spending lots of time just being together—not *accomplishing* something. God's refining work in us—such as the forming of patience, endurance, and perseverance—also offers no immediate payback. Yet these things keep coming up in Scripture as valuable, even if they are born of "wasted" time.

Traditional time-management techniques won't spring us from the busyness trap. Squeezing still more tasks into still less time will fill our calendars, but it won't fill our souls. Best heed the counsel of one Mr. Thomas Blague, who, in 1603, preached to King James: "Blessed therefore is the man, which walketh not after the counsel of pragmatic and busy heads."[11]

The deeper concern must not be how we manage our time in a busy world but how we manage *our inner world* in a busy time.

The Tranquility Solution

The solution to the busyness trap is not to try to do it all but to discern what God wants us to do, in the way and at the time God wants us to do it, and to trust him with the rest. This is the tranquility solution, which we'll unfold over the remaining chapters of this book.

The tranquility solution	Do what *God* wants you to do, and trust *him* with the rest.

In the early years of the Italian Renaissance, painters like Michelangelo were often commissioned to paint enormous murals. The best method they found was fresco painting, applying the colors right onto a wet plaster wall. The paint and the plaster dried together, preserving the crisp, vivid colors.

But it wasn't possible to plaster and paint an entire wall in one day. All that could be done was one small part of the whole. If the artist was painting the background of a mural, he could possibly complete a stretch of wall ten feet by ten feet. But if he was working on the details of, say, a bouquet of pink gladiolas, he might work morning to night on a section no larger than a dinner plate.

So each morning, the painter mixed up a small bucket of plaster and then coated the portion of the wall that he believed he would be able to finish before the sun went down. And that small portion of the whole wall was called the *giornatta*, the "day-piece," the work that could be done in a day.

Isn't that a beautiful metaphor for the work of our days? Our lives are not the sum of our crowded to-do lists but great blank stretches of wall. And the Master Painter desires to take that space—the span of our three score years and ten—and transform it into a masterpiece. Some days he may want to do an expansive work, to work in and through us in momentous ways, leading us in such a way that broad strokes go out from our work of the day and touch dozens of others. Other days his interest may be in doing only a small, quiet work on our interior. The work is wholly his to determine.

This is our privilege and responsibility: to begin each day by relinquishing the brush to the Master, for the masterpiece is not

ours to paint but his. That often leads me to lift up a prayer as
dawn cracks open the sky and throws its colors against the world:

> Lord, what would you have of me today? My life belongs to you.
> Hold sway over me. Make me open to your Spirit and available for
> your purposes. Lead me today in my *giornatta*. I pray this for your
> sake and for your glory. Amen.

ONE HANDFUL
WITH TRANQUILITY

5

Deep Time

Time is the stuff life is made of.

Benjamin Franklin,
Poor Richard's Almanac

I have measured out my life with coffee spoons.

T. S. Eliot, "The Love Song of J. Alfred Prufrock"

We concern ourselves with the skin of time rather than its heart. . . . Listening for the chimes, we fail to hear the clock.

Robert Grudin, *Time and the Art of Living*

The world promises the trifles of time. I promise the high things of eternity.

Thomas à Kempis, *The Imitation of Christ*

Live deep instead of fast.

Henry Seidel Canby

Redemption measures all my time.

George Herbert, "H. Baptism (I)"

We were with friends in the mountains of Colorado for a shared family vacation when our host received a phone

59

call. It was her sister, a non-Christian in the middle of a painful divorce. As our friend took the call, the rest of us, knowing something of her sister's circumstances, prayed for the conversation.

More than an hour later, our friend returned, grinning wide. At first, she told us, the conversation had tiptoed along on the surface. Then, as sometimes happens in the providence of God, it had unexpectedly plunged into a discussion about the things that matter most. Our friend was able to explore with her sister what it could mean for her to experience the love and acceptance of God in the middle of this relational devastation.

When the conversation entered that deeper level, our friend prayed silently that she would say the right things—enough but not too much, "because," as she said, "those are such fragile and holy moments."

God visits earth in moments just like that one all the time. Suddenly an ordinary pocket of time, like a stocking on Christmas morning, is stretched beyond recognition. As we step into it, we discover it is crammed with divine presence and purpose and potential—a holy and fragile moment.

Years after that conversation, I spoke with the sister at a wedding. She thanked me for my prayers during that confusing time and told me how God drew her to him in the years that followed. We were both in tears as she described his transforming power and presence in her life today.

Extraordinary Time

In an earlier chapter, I introduced the two Greek words for "time," *kairos* and *chronos*. Let's explore these words more deeply now.

The word *chronos*, from which we derive our word *chronological*, suggests the steady, paced unfolding of time: one hour, one day, one year, one generation, each followed by the next, none different from the next or the previous.[1] This is ordinary time measured out by the dispassionate hands of a clock or the inflexible grid of a calendar.

Kairos, on the other hand, is time freighted with significance, moments laden with momentousness. While the semantic ranges of the two words overlap, each has its own nuance. When writers chose *kairos* over *chronos*, they often wished to speak not just of any moment but of a decisive or crucial one.[2] Used this way, *kairos* is extraordinary time, amplified time, crossroads time, hinge time.

When I was a kid, my grandfather would tuck pieces of candy in his pockets before he came to visit, special treats for us to discover and savor. *Kairos* time is *chronos* time with treats in its pockets.

This secular Greek idea of *kairos* served the writers of the New Testament beautifully in describing a view of the universe in which a personal God is the Author of events in time. He is above and amid all things, the fashioner of moments imbued with meaning and opportunity. In the hands of the New Testament authors, *kairos* moments are times made extraordinary by the presence and purposes of God, puncture points when God intrudes and confronts us with himself.

Kairos moments are Jacob's-ladder moments (Gen. 28:12), divinely ordained rips in the seam of day-to-day life when we are confronted with the holy purposes of God. Heaven and earth kiss in *kairos* moments.

Such moments demand a decision or compel an action.[3] They come to us as both gift and insistence. *Kairos* moments require both that they be recognized and that their urgings be answered. Our ability to do so draws us deeper into God's love and closer to his will, while our inability moves us away from God's intentions and toward God's judgment.

For those who walk through a *kairos* moment uncomprehendingly, the saddest of indictments comes in the words of T. S. Eliot: "We had the experience but missed the meaning."[4]

The Hinge Moment

The New Testament uses the word *kairos* to refer to two experiences of God puncturing human existence. The first is *the* defining moment of all time: the incarnation. Mary gave birth not merely to a Savior but to an age. This is the fulcrum in human history, the center of time,[5] the hinge moment by which God closes one era and introduces another.[6] In the fullness of *chronos* (Gal. 4:4) came the ultimate *kairos* moment—*Kairos* with a capital *K*, if you will.

Announcing the start of his public ministry as Messiah, Jesus says, "The *kairos* has come" (Mark 1:15). With these inaugural words—the first that come from Jesus's mouth in Mark's Gospel account—Jesus rends the fabric of existence and proclaims the in-breaking of the kingdom of God.

All the more poignant, then, are the words with which Jesus brings his public ministry to an end. On his sad trek to Jerusalem in the final days of his ministry, he crests the ridgeline on the Jericho road, looks down into the city, and breaks into tears, crying out, "If you, even you, had only known on this day what would bring you peace—but now it is hidden from your eyes. The days will come upon you when your enemies will build an embankment against you and encircle you and hem you in on every side. They will dash you to the ground, you and the children within your walls. They will not leave one stone on another, because you did not recognize the *kairos* of God's coming to you" (Luke 19:42–44).

How telling that, when Herod cross-examines the Magi regarding when the child king was born, he probes for year-month-week-day time: "Herod called the Magi secretly and found out from them the exact *chronos* the star had appeared" (Matt. 2:7). He cannot see (or perhaps sees but refuses to acknowledge) the deeper significance of this event—the *kairos* of God's coming.

The word *kairos* is used in speaking of the entire cluster of events surrounding the first coming, such as the fulfillment of God's prophetic declarations in John's birth (Luke 1:20), Jesus's power over the demonic realm (Matt. 8:29), and the crucifixion (Matt. 26:18; John 7:6; Rom. 3:26; 5:6; 1 Tim. 2:6). The word is also used to describe the *second* coming and related events, when Jesus will return as conquering King and Judge at the close of the age. We see the word in conjunction with the rise of the antichrist (2 Thess. 2:6), the coming of the Son of Man on the clouds (Mark 13:33; Rev. 22:10), the last judgment (1 Cor. 4:5; 1 Pet. 4:17; Rev. 11:18), and the close of the age (Matt. 21:34; 1 Pet. 1:5). The first visitation God brought about "at the proper *kairos*" (1 Tim. 2:6), and the second "God will bring about in his own *kairos*" (1 Tim. 6:15).

As the opening chapter of John's Gospel makes clear—"though the world was made through him, the world did not recognize him" (John 1:10)—what by some was identified as an extraordinary moment was by others mistaken as yet another bit of ordinary time.

Just a couple of days ago, I sat wonder-struck in front of Caravaggio's *Supper at Emmaus* (1601). Caravaggio portrays the risen Jesus at the moment he breaks the bread, and the eyes of Cleopas and his companion are opened to recognize him (Luke 24:30–31). Jesus sits in the center of the painting, eyes down, serene, one hand reaching toward the viewer to draw him gently in. On either side are the two disciples. One flings his arms wide in astonishment, openmouthed, staring; the other, head jutting forward, eyebrows arched in wonder, shoves himself up from his seat. For these two, this is a *kairos* moment. God in the flesh, risen from the dead, is present with them!

But at Jesus's right shoulder stands another man, the innkeeper, thumbs tucked confidently into his belt, a casual lean to his stance. He looks on the scene with disinterest. For him, this is a mere *chronos* moment. Just another Sunday evening. Just another customer.

Faced with God in the person of Jesus, each of us is called to *recognition* (God is indeed present and moving in this moment), *decision* (I will give him my allegiance), and *action* (I will do whatever he requires of me). Doing so secures for us the kingdom. Failure to do so brings judgment and separation from God.

Puncture Points

The first use of the word *kairos*, then, relates specifically to the twin missions from heaven when God visits earth in the flesh, puncturing human history.

The second use of the word—what we might call *kairos* with a small *k*—refers to the myriad ways God punctures *our* history, breaking into our lives again and again during this era between the first and second comings.

Yesterday, Andrew, our director of ministries, was reflective as he tried to describe a conversation he'd had with his ailing mother-in-law the day before. They had talked about the things that matter most of all: her relationship with God, hope in Christ, eternal security. But it wasn't merely a conversation. "All I can say is God visited us. It was a holy moment." Andrew's eyes widened and he leaned forward, earnest. "Do you ever have the sense that this is real? I mean really *real*? These are the truest things of all. God really is with us. He really does want to spend eternity with us. He really has prepared a place for us. God really is serious about completing what he began in us!"

This wasn't a moment of Andrew reviewing the facts of his faith. This was a visit from the One in whom his faith resides.

As followers of Christ, we expect and invite God's involvement in our day-to-day lives. We ask him, among other things (following the pattern of the Lord's Prayer), to bring glory to his holy name, advance his kingdom, carry out his will in and through us, meet our daily needs, forgive our repeated failings, and protect us from the schemes of the evil one. *Kairos* moments are the window moments in which God gives us a glimpse of him doing these very things.

That "random" call. That "chance" conversation. That person on our heart. That unanticipated gift. That unexpected confrontation. That unforeseen crisis. That familiar passage of Scripture. That strange turn of events. That invitation from out of the blue. That inner stirring. That whispered prompting. That persistent prodding. That word of grace. A *kairos* moment.

Kairos moments are moments of unaccounted generosity that we are called simply to receive with gratitude. At the same time, they require of us the same faith response as when this world was first confronted with Jesus incarnate: recognition (God is present and moving in our midst now), decision (I will say yes to his invitation in this moment), and action (I will do whatever he requires of me).

One of the most memorable examples of this faith perspective in Scripture is the moment when enemies of the exiled Jews persuade the Persian king Xerxes to issue a decree declaring that all Jews in the kingdom should be put to death. Now it "happens" that a beautiful Jewish woman named Esther has been chosen to be part of the king's harem and is then elevated to the role of queen. Mordecai, Esther's adoptive father, urges her "to go into the king's presence to beg for mercy and plead with him for her people" (Esther 4:8). When she demurs, reminding him that it is against the law to seek audience with the king unless summoned and that she could be killed for this affront, Mordecai challenges her: "Who knows but that you have come to your royal position for such a time as this?" (4:14).

Kairos moments. Such-a-time-as-this moments. God is afoot.

Pirouettes in Time

Three weeks ago, while we were away on vacation, our daughter's car was stolen from in front of our house. Detectives were called in and soon put their finger on the culprit—a young man I knew from church. Taking advantage of a moment of unsupervised access to our home, he had slipped in and grabbed a set of keys. Later that night, he had returned and driven off in the car. Having left a pretty obvious trail of evidence, he eventually confessed to the detectives, not only to this theft but to another as well.

The recipient of a four-year, full-ride scholarship, this young man was to begin college in a few weeks. Now all that was in jeopardy. A conviction for this crime would erase the scholarship and probably any thought of ever attending college. Worse, it would send him careening along the path of his father before him, whose footsteps now paced a prison cell.

At his hearing, I was asked if I had anything I wished to say. I turned to face the young man.

"God puts before each of us moments that come filled with great opportunity and great responsibility. This is one of those moments in your life. We are eager for this to be a redemptive moment in your life. We as the victims are willing to withhold judgment on this case. That would keep this theft from your record and allow you to go to college. This is an amazing opportunity for you, a chance to begin a new life. But this moment comes with great responsibility: to own up to what you have done, to resolve never to steal again, and to become honest and God-honoring. Don't miss what this moment requires of you."

When we met again two weeks later, I handed him a book I'd bought for him and asked him to read the first two chapters. The opening encounter of *Les Miserables* is one of the finest moments in all of literature.

Jean Valjean, a convict on parole, steals the silver of a bishop who has graciously given him shelter for the night. But he is caught by village gendarmes as he tries to escape and is dragged back to the *monseigneur*. The police tell him that Valjean claims he was given the silver and demand to know if that is true.

The clergyman confirms Valjean's story. Then he walks to the mantelpiece, picks up the silver candlesticks, and hands them to the astonished Valjean. "Have you forgotten that I gave you the candlesticks as well? They're made of silver like the rest, and worth a good two hundred francs. Did you forget to take them?"

The bishop sees the gendarmes to the door with thanks. Then he turns back to Valjean, leans close to him, and says in a low voice:

"Do not forget, never forget, that you have promised to use this money in becoming an honest man."

Jean Valjean, who had no recollection of ever having promised anything, remained speechless. The Bishop had emphasized the words when he uttered them. He resumed with solemnity:—

"Jean Valjean, my brother, you no longer belong to evil, but to good. It is your soul that I buy from you; I withdraw it from black thoughts and the spirit of perdition, and I give it to God."[7]

This proves to be the turning point of Valjean's life, as the rest of the novel so beautifully captures. May it be so as well for the young man who stole our car.

Our culture is obsessed with managing time. But we're preoccupied with managing the *chronos*: our minutes and hours and days.

For people of the kingdom, time management of a different sort is required: *kairos* management. For God has not merely placed us in time; he has promised to encounter us in it. He has designs upon it. Our dealings with time have to take account of this.

Accordingly, the biblical witness invites us into three practices: understanding the *kairos*, making the most of the *kairos*, and trusting God with the rest. The exploration of these will be the focus of the remainder of this book.

Understanding the Times

6

While There Is Time

O late late late, late is the time.

T. S. Eliot, *Murder in the Cathedral*

What is the time? Never mind, it's not important.

last words of János Arany

And so there we all were on a little wave of time lifting up to eternity, and none of us ever in time would know what to make of it. How could we? It is a mystery, for we are eternal beings living in time.

Wendell Berry, *Jayber Crow*

How few, how short these hours my heart must beat—then on, into the real world where the unseen becomes important.

journal entry by Jim Elliot

"I wish it need not have happened in my time," said Frodo.

"So do I," said Gandalf, "and so do all who live to see such times. But that is not for them to decide. All we have to decide is what to do with the time that is given us."

J. R. R. Tolkien, *The Fellowship of the Ring*

71

My wife and two of her friends went to a conference for pastors' wives in Colorado. When they got to the Denver airport for the trip home, they had so much margin that they decided to grab a bite to eat before they went to their gate.

As Sharon tells the story, the three were sitting at the table, engrossed in conversation. At one point, it occurred to Sharon to glance at her watch. When she saw what time it was, she leapt to her feet. Their flight left in less than half an hour! The three grabbed their bags and ran.

First, they had to negotiate a long line at security. Then there was the endless tram ride to their terminal, followed by the long walk to their gate. They reached their gate, breathless, with moments to spare—and it was empty. Even the clerk's counter was unmanned. They double-checked the gate number. Right gate.

Then one of them noticed that the plane still sat at the end of the Jetway. They sprang into action. Sharon banged on the door. Anne jiggled the door handle. And Amanda stood in front of the window, waving frantically in the hope that the pilots would see her and . . . what? Shut down their preflight procedures, reopen the cabin door, roll the Jetway back in place, and reopen the gate for three desperate women?

The plane hadn't pulled away, but the deadline for boarding had long since passed and the gate was closed. It was too late.

Nightfall

I was struck recently by the urgency of the biblical writers who press us to act *while there is time*. I came across it as I was memorizing Psalm 32 during Lent a few years ago.

> Let the godly pray to you while there is still time,
>   that they may not drown in the floodwaters of judgment. (v. 6 NLT)

Just around the corner, in the book of Joel, I encountered the phrase again:

> Turn to me now, while there is time.
> Give me your hearts. (2:12 NLT)

Jesus's teaching is suffused with references to that same approaching threshold, pointing to a coming time when things will be markedly different than they are now. He refers to the present redemptive era as a rapidly fading day. It is already dusk, he says, and once it becomes night, it will be too late to respond, whether in belief or action. Here are a few examples:

> We must quickly carry out the tasks assigned us by the one who sent us. The night is coming and then no one can work. (John 9:4 NLT)

> My light will shine for you just a little longer. Walk in the light while you can, so the darkness will not overtake you. (John 12:35–36 NLT)

> When the master of the house has locked the door, it will be too late. (Luke 13:25 NLT)

The same urgency figures in Paul's writings. Interestingly, Paul reverses Jesus's analogy: the night is coming to an end and soon it will be day.

> You know how late it is; time is running out [literally: Do this, *understanding the present time*]. Wake up, for our salvation is nearer now than when we first believed. The night is almost gone; the day of salvation will soon be here. So remove your dark deeds like dirty clothes, and put on the shining armor of right living. Because we belong to the day, we must live decent lives for all to see. (Rom. 13:11–13 NLT)

His letter to the Corinthian church is equally urgent in calling us to be about the things that matter while there is time:

The time that remains is very short. So from now on, those with wives should not focus only on their marriage. Those who weep or who rejoice or who buy things should not be absorbed by their weeping or their joy or their possessions. Those who use the things of the world should not become attached to them. For this world as we know it will soon pass away. (1 Cor. 7:29–31 NLT)

Both Jesus and Paul urge us to live mindful of the era in which we find ourselves. Our clear understanding of the times, our knowing which season we are in and what it requires of us, is crucial to faithfully fulfilling our calling as followers of Christ in this life.

I'm reminded of the urgency of the squirrels in our backyard as they harvest acorns from our pin oak. Creation has announced to the squirrels, "Summer has come to an end, and winter is nearly upon us." Those squirrels understand. If they want to enjoy acorns this winter, it is now or not at all. Now is the time.

What Day Is It?

If we look at God's dealings with humanity over time, we see in the witness of the Bible four great eras of human history. In his *Centuries of Meditation*, the seventeenth-century poet Thomas Traherne defines them as man's "fourfold estate of innocency, misery, grace, and glory."[1]

Innocency

The first era began with creation. The Hebrew word often used to describe this first chapter of human history is *shalom*. Things were in every way just as God intended them to be. God as King ruled over willing and joyful subjects. There was no pain in the world, no loss, nothing broken. All was as God purposed; wholeness prevailed.

Adam and Eve lived in immediate and unrestricted intimacy with God. They took unhurried delight in him. The most urgent requirement was simply to enjoy him and his gifts: the provision of this beautiful, bountiful world and the gift of one another.

Misery

All of that changed in a moment when willing and joyful subjects became willful. Adam and Eve denounced God, refusing his rightful place on the throne of their lives. They usurped his legitimate rule and rebelled against him. In that moment, creation was marred, and the kingdom collapsed into anarchy as the subjects rebelled against the King and now lived each for himself.

This second era was marked by distance from God, as God drove Adam and Eve out of his holy presence. Chaos and brokenness were introduced into a world now marked by sin, pain, and loss. Life was difficult, and God was far away.

At the same time, in this era hope was born, as God through his prophets inspired words that promised a coming Prince of Peace, the Messiah, who would put this broken world to rights.

This second era, then, was a time to lament the cost of humanity's rebellion against God but also a time to wait in eager expectancy for the promised Deliverer.

Grace

Then came the *kairos* moment, the hinge in history, when creation was reclaimed and the kingdom was inaugurated. God came to earth in human form. Jesus revealed God through every word and deed.

God kept his promise. We are no longer alone. God is with us; intimacy with God has been restored. Those who recognize Jesus and believe in him he makes right with God through his death. As the risen Lord, he restores them to their rightful place under

God's loving rule as willing, joyful subjects. For these followers, the old has passed away and the new has come.

Yet in this third era, life remains profoundly difficult. While our interiors begin to be put right, the world is yet marked by brokenness, scarred by the presence of pain, sin, and loss. But hope persists, for God has promised that *all* things will be made new one day.

This is the season in which we now live. This season between the two comings of Christ is "the *kairos* of God's favor" (2 Cor. 6:2). These days between the first appearance of Jesus in humility and his second in triumph are crowned with the grace and patience of the Mighty One, as Peter reminds us: "He is patient with you, not wanting anyone to perish, but everyone to come to repentance. . . . Our Lord's patience means salvation" (2 Pet. 3:9, 15).

But we would be mistaken to allow ourselves to be lulled by the patience of God into spiritual apathy or missional indifference. This pocket of time will not last. "The *kairos* is short," Paul warns (1 Cor. 7:29). Now is the time—in this short breath between his coming in the cave and his coming on the clouds—for us to be reconciled to God, and now is the time for us to help others be reconciled to God.

Glory

During his years of ministry on earth, Jesus made it clear that one day he will return to earth and close out the age. He warned that his return will be sudden and unexpected: "You do not know when that *kairos* will come" (Mark 13:33).

At his second coming, human history will come to an end. In fulfillment of his promises, God's kingdom will be fully established, sin and death will be done away with, and there will be no more pain or tears. All will be made new; wholeness will be restored.

At the cusp between the age of grace and the age of glory, each person will stand in judgment before God. For those who wanted nothing to do with God during the *kairos* of grace, God will honor their decision and consign them to an eternity of painful separation from him. But those who have put their confidence in the risen Jesus and submitted to his loving rule will enter into an eternity of intimacy with God, unending days in which to enjoy God, the new world, and one another.[2]

Let me use an analogy to capture the essence of each age.

Imagine that morning dawns with your family happily together in your home. You are joyful, content, and at peace, enjoying the sweetness of one another's company. This parallels the first stage of redemptive history.

Not long after daybreak, a tornado hits. Your home is destroyed, and you and your family are swept from the house and driven apart, scattered by the wind and buried under debris. But even as you suffer, word reaches you that your father has promised to come and find you. You are trapped, hurting, and afraid, but you endure and wait for rescue. This is like the second redemptive stage.

In the afternoon, the eldest son eventually makes his way to where you have been buried by the tornado. He comes from your father's side to rescue you and to bring you home. But first, once he has dug you out and tended to your wounds, he asks you to help look for the other children who are still lost, to join him in bringing them back to your father as well. You are limping with pain, but you are filled with joy because you have been rescued, and you enter wholeheartedly into the work of search and rescue while it is still day. This is the third stage.

Finally, as night falls, with every member of the family rescued, the family gathers again in a new home and closes the door to the darkness. The rescued enjoy the father's love, one another's presence, rest, and peace ever after. This corresponds to the final stage of redemptive history.

We were called—we were made—to live in the love of God our Father and in the care of our Lord Jesus Christ (see Jude 1:1). This is indeed our experience in the first of the four redemptive eras. In the second, it is stripped from us, but we retain its promise; in the third, we taste its sweetness intermingled with the bitterness of life in a fallen world; in the final era, it becomes our experience fully and for all time.

Wrong Time Zone

Think back to that phrase earlier in this chapter: "while there is time." Where we are in time matters. If we misunderstand the times in which we live, our living will be markedly out of step with what is happening around us, to our great detriment.

Here are some ways we can lose track of our surroundings in time and miss the requirements of the moment, just as Sharon and her friends did at the airport restaurant.

If we forget that God's work of rescue is not yet complete, that there is more saving to be done in us and more to be done in this world of ours, we may fall into thinking we should experience in *this* era that which will not be fully ours until the *next*, wrongly looking for fulfillment here on earth. Thinking of ourselves as already home, we will want to trade in our temporary visas for green cards and claim the rest and comfort that can only really be ours in the next. We forget that ours is a pilgrim status, that we are, as David says, "a traveler passing through" (Ps. 39:12 NLT).

A related mistake is to let up before the end of the race, wrongly thinking that, because God's redemptive work has already encompassed us, it must be largely done. *I* have already crossed the finished line. Grace has come to *me*. *I* am right with God. What else is left? Losing sight of God's equal regard for the spiritual well-being of those around us, we can easily miss the strategic urgency of these short days between Jesus's visits and fall into complacency concerning others. But the race is not finished. These are not days of spiritual leisure. Rather, these are days of fruitful labor, of rigorous witness and service; rest will be ours in the age to come (Phil. 1:22).

If we forget that the pain and brokenness of the previous era carry over into this one, we may be shaken in our faith when we experience devastating loss or debilitating sin. How could God let this happen? Doesn't he love me? Isn't he all-powerful? Why won't God keep his promises? If we expect God's redemptive work to find its full expression in this life, our confidence in God may be shattered when we experience evidence to the contrary. Life and hope will not perfectly align until Christ's return (Rom. 8:24–25).

Similarly, if we confuse God's having *begun* a good work in us with his having carried it through to completion, if we think we should have "arrived" spiritually in these days on earth instead of having to wait for our graduation into perfection, if we think the victorious Christian life means uncompromised holiness or un-qualified Christlikeness or unwavering peace today, we may despair of our sanctification or even our salvation. Scripture reminds us that these are the days of overcoming, not of triumphing—arduous days of persevering and enduring and clinging to hope until God's redemptive work is completed (Rev. 2:3, 7).

Thomas à Kempis reflects this when he writes:

> The days of this time are few and evil, full of sorrows and pressing trials; where a man is soiled by many sins, snared by many passions, shackled by many fears, torn apart by many cares, distracted by many questionings, tangled with worthless things, crowded round by many errors, worn by many toils, burdened by temptations, weakened by pleasures, and tortured by want.
>
> When will there be peace well-founded, peace beyond dis-turbance and care, peace within and without, peace on all sides

established? Good Jesus, when shall I stand to look upon you? When shall I gaze upon the glory of your kingdom? When will you be all in all to me? O, when shall I be with you in your kingdom, which you have prepared for those that love you from eternity? I am left a poor exile on hostile soil amid daily wars and the direst misfortunes.[3]

He understood the times.

In the four chapters that follow, we'll explore further what it means for us, in practical terms, to read the times correctly.

7

The Circle and the Arrow

La vita vola. Life flies.

Italian proverb

Life has a double motion—straight and bent: one eye on this
earth, one eye on heaven.

George Herbert, "Colossians 3:3"

Time! What an empty vapor 'tis
And days how swift they are;
Swift as an Indian arrow—
Fly on like a shooting star.

Abraham Lincoln
as a schoolboy

Time flies like an arrow.
Fruit flies like a banana.

Anthony Oettinger,
"The Uses of Computing
in Science"

Time hangs on us awkwardly, like someone else's clothes. Why?
In part because our lives straddle two realms. We are temporal

beings, bound to time like a kite to string. "He marked out their appointed times in history and the boundaries of their lands" (Acts 17:26). But we are also eternal beings, the outer reaches of our lives stretching beyond any boundary of time. "He has also set eternity in the human heart" (Eccles. 3:11).

Born into finite time but made for time everlasting, we walk this world awkwardly, like skiers in ski boots tramping through the ski lodge, better fitted for the gliding bliss of the slopes outside. Surely some of our tension with time finds its source here. Sheldon Vanauken, the author of *A Severe Mercy*, reflects on our conundrum:

> Not only are we harried by time, we seem unable for a thousand generations even to get used to it. We are always amazed at it—how fast it goes, how slowly it goes, how much of it is gone. Where, we cry, has the time gone? We aren't adapted to it, not at home in it. If that is so, it may appear as a proof, or at least a powerful suggestion, that eternity exists and is our home.[1]

Two jarringly different experiences of time—the now and the forever—stride like alternating footfalls through our lives.

Under-the-Sun Time

From within our earthbound point of view as human beings, we generally experience time as circular. Time is a cycle of events that is endlessly repeating: a succession of moments and days and weeks and months and years and lifetimes, all in endless repetition.

"Are you serious?" I look at my ministry assistant in disbelief. "Already?" The calendar is open in front of her, and her pencil tip taps lightly on the little box with the 15 in the corner.

"Don't tell me two months have gone by!" I'm baffled. It seems like just three days ago I was trying to figure out what to write for the *last* newsletter. "Again?"

Again. Time to get my hair cut, time to get my teeth cleaned, time to change the oil, time to pay the bills, time to head back to school, time to get up and go to work. Again.

We experience time's circular nature in the seasons. Spring blooms out of winter dormancy; then the full growth of summer arrives, followed by the golden days of autumn harvest, and all too soon it is winter again.

Cyclical time is evident in the phases of the moon, as it changes from new to gibbous to full and back over the course of a month, a cycle echoed by the monthly changes in a woman's body. The stages of a life reveal a similar circular pattern. We are born and grow and age and die, the same cycle that our parents went through before us and our children will go through after us. Around and around and around.

On top of these endlessly repeating natural rhythms and cycles are others of our own making. We have regular meals. We have daily routines (make the bed, read the paper, walk the dog). We have weekly housework rituals and a certain weekend rhythm. We speak of the school year and football season. And we recognize a host of annual events and celebrations: birthdays, anniversaries, holidays, the Grammys, the Oscars, April 15, the Indy 500, the fashion issues, and so on.

This is time "under the sun," a favorite expression of the writer of Ecclesiastes, who uses it more than thirty times to describe life from earth's point of view. This is day-to-day, *terra firma* time.

Four qualities in particular are true of under-the-sun time.

Laborious

Life never seems to let up. Again and again in the book of Ecclesiastes we hear the theme:

I hated life, because the work that is done under the sun was grievous to me. All of it is meaningless, a chasing after the wind. (2:17)

So my heart began to despair over all my toilsome labor under
the sun. (2:20)

What do people get for all the toil and anxious striving with which
they labor under the sun? (2:22)

All their days their work is grief and pain; even at night their minds
do not rest. This too is meaningless. (2:23)

In part physically, due to the work it requires, and in part emo-
tionally, because of its never-ending nature, under-the-sun time is
overhung with a pall of weariness. Ecclesiastes's opening chapter
conveys (in its words and its seesaw rhythm) a sense of our being
trapped in, and sapped by, time's restless repetition.

> Generations come and generations go,
>   but the earth remains forever.
> The sun rises and the sun sets,
>   and hurries back to where it rises.
> The wind blows to the south
>   and turns to the north;
>   round and round it goes,
>   ever returning on its course.
> All streams flow into the sea,
>   yet the sea is never full.
> To the place the streams come from,
>   there they return again.
> All things are wearisome,
>   more than one can say.
> The eye never has enough of seeing,
>   nor the ear its fill of hearing.
> What has been will be again,
>   what has been done will be done again;
>   there is nothing new under the sun. (Eccles. 1:4–9)

One of our neighbors owns a dog named Ferris. Ferris is a bit, well, different. When he's let out of the house, he runs in circles around the front yard, following the same path every time. To the neighbors' house on the right, turn, to the sidewalk, turn, to the neighbors' house on the left, turn, to the corner of the yard, turn, and so on. He's begun to wear a path into the grass. Pouring rain or blazing sun, on he goes, running in circles incessantly until he is called inside.

Around and around we go too, the same weary foot treads over the same worn soil. Such is time as we experience it day to day.

Fleeting

Life under the sun is not only wearying and laborious; it is fleeting as well. "How Sunday into Monday melts!" Ogden Nash is said to have quipped.

In Chutes-and-Ladders fashion, we fall into the front end of a routine and suddenly find ourselves at the other end, with no memory of what happened in between. The time has come and gone, and we can't remember for the life of us where we've just been. This wormhole experience of time contributes to its fleeting quality.

The themes of time's rapidity and life's brevity surface often in the Bible. For instance, David prays, "LORD, remind me how brief my time on earth will be. Remind me that my days are numbered— how fleeting my life is. You have made my life no longer than the width of my hand. My entire lifetime is just a moment to you; at best, each of us is but a breath. We are merely moving shadows, and all our busy rushing ends in nothing" (Ps. 39:4–6 NLT).

Moses expresses alarm at the same idea: "You sweep people away in the sleep of death—they are like the new grass of the morning: In the morning it springs up new, but by evening it is dry and withered. . . . Our days may come to seventy years, or eighty, if our strength endures; yet the best of them are trouble and sorrow, for they quickly pass, and we fly away. . . . Teach us to number our days, that we may gain a heart of wisdom" (Ps. 90:5–6, 10, 12; see also Ps. 103).

And Job laments, "My days are swifter than a weaver's shuttle, and they come to an end without hope. Remember, O God, that my life is but a breath" (Job 7:6–7; see also 9:25–26; 14:1–2).

Meaningless

The writer of Ecclesiastes repeatedly uses the Hebrew word *hebel* to describe life under the sun. The word means "the merest breath," "an exhale," "a puff of air"—and, by extension, "meaninglessness." This is the third quality that marks under-the-sun time. "*Hebel! Hebel!*" "'Meaningless! Meaningless!' says the Teacher. 'Utterly meaningless! Everything is meaningless!'" (Eccles. 1:2). Much of life feels shorn of meaning: its inequities, the difficulties of work, the transitory nature of riches, the inadequacy of pleasure, the unsatisfying results of achievement, and the certainty of death eclipse its radiant purpose.

The movie *Groundhog Day* asks a thought-provoking question: What would happen if we were stuck in the same day, endlessly repeating, day after day after day? The protagonist, played by comedian Bill Murray, is shocked and disoriented to discover he is trapped in a single recurring day, and he tries to find a way out. Then, realizing there is no escape, he falls into self-indulgence and hedonism, calculatingly using his knowledge of how the day will unfold to indulge his selfish desires without regard for others. This, however, proves hollow. Eventually, as the same day follows upon itself in lengthening repetition, he feels trapped and despairs of life. He wakes each day with the resolve to bring his life—and the new day with it—to a hasty end. Only after months of repeating the same day, first in seeking escape, then in seeking pleasure, then in seeking relief, does he wonder if there might not be some meaning to be found outside of his own small self—an impulse that becomes the means of his redemption.

God-Forsaken

Finally, for all practical purposes, under-the-sun time is time from which God seems absent. The writer of Ecclesiastes parades before us what seems to be the God-forgotten randomness of life:

I have seen something else under the sun:

> The race is not to the swift
>> or the battle to the strong,
> nor does food come to the wise
>> or wealth to the brilliant
>> or favor to the learned;
> but time and chance happen to them all.

Moreover, no one knows when their hour will come:

> As fish are caught in a cruel net,
>> or birds are taken in a snare,
> so people are trapped by evil times
>> that fall unexpectedly upon them. (9:11–12)

From our earthly vantage point, life seems simply to happen, with no hand fashioning its unfolding. That seeming arbitrariness of existence leads some to wonder where God is (Ps. 79:10), or if he even exists (Ps. 14:1). David sums up the God-forsaken feel of life under the sun when he groans, "My prayers returned to me unanswered" (Ps. 35:13).

Fully half of the psalms are laments in response to God's seeming disengagement or absence. Life under the sun drives us to ask:

My God, my God, why have you forsaken me? (Ps. 22:1)

How long will you hide your face from me? (Ps. 13:1)

Why, LORD, do you stand far off? (Ps. 10:1)

How long, LORD, will you look on? (Ps. 35:17)

> Why, Lord, do you reject me and hide your face from me?
> (Ps. 88:14)

This can lead us into an outlook more consistent with superstition than with faith. As an example, when things are going well, we can become anxious about the inevitability that "the other shoe will drop" and that the happy circumstances we're enjoying will be stripped away. Life seems to be ordered by happenstance, not by a loving God.

The fleetingness of time, the weariness of life, and the absence of God are brought together in Psalm 89 when Ethan writes, "How long, Lord? Will you hide yourself forever? . . . Remember how fleeting is my life. For what futility you have created all humanity!" (vv. 46–47).

Such is our experience of life under the sun. But there is, by the grace of God, another vantage point.

Time on High

Time is viewed from another perspective in the Bible as well. We could call this "heavenward" time—time as God sees it from the perspective of heaven.

The New Testament uses the simplest of words to capture this vantage point. *Anō*, meaning "upward," "above," or "heavenward," was a favorite expression of both John and Paul. The word points to the home of the Father and the Son, the source of all wisdom and knowledge, and the goal and destination of every follower of Christ.

> The one who comes from *anō* is above all; the one who is from the earth belongs to the earth, and speaks as one from the earth. (John 3:31)

> You are from below; I am from *anō*. You are of this world; I am not of this world. (John 8:23)

Then Jesus looked *anō* and said, "Father, I thank you that you have heard me." (John 11:41)

Since, then, you have been raised with Christ, set your hearts on things *anō*, where Christ is, seated at the right hand of God. Set your minds on things *anō*, not on earthly things. (Col. 3:1–2)

But one thing I do: Forgetting what is behind and straining toward what is ahead, I press on toward the goal to win the prize for which God has called me *anō* in Christ Jesus. (Phil. 3:13–14)

When we contrast under-the-sun time with heavenward time, we're not talking about two different time zones—Earth Standard and Heaven Central—but rather time on earth as seen from two wildly different vantage points: one that includes God and his purposes and the other that excludes them.

From this *anō* perspective—from the vantage point of God's throne—time is forward-facing and unfaltering, marked by an unswerving linearity, not a circle but a line, like an arrow whisking inexorably toward its target.

If the characteristic exclamation of under-the-sun time is "Again?" that of heavenward time is "Finally!"

Apocalypse Now

We see heavenward time most clearly in a book in which precious little may seem clear to us at first: the book of Revelation. The book is split between two perspectives. The first three chapters capture the earthbound vantage point we talked about earlier in this chapter, as John and his fellow believers find themselves pressed down under the crippling weight of persecution and hardship.

We're brought, especially in the second and third chapters, into the conditions under which the churches of Asia Minor struggled at the end of the first century. They are suffering physically and economically (2:9–10). Some have caved in under the unending pressure to renounce Christ, compromising morally (2:20) or spiritually (2:14–16). Others have fallen away from Christ altogether (3:1–2). But some have managed to endure and not grow weary, holding fast to their faith (2:3) in spite of unrelenting persecution. This is a portrait of the exhausting struggle of life under the sun.

Then, at the start of chapter 4, John is swept up into heaven. A heavenly voice says to John, "'Come up here, and I will show you what must take place after this.' At once I was in the Spirit, and there before me was a throne in heaven with someone sitting on it" (4:1–2).

The throne, the seat of authority and command, expresses God's rule over all the realm of heaven and earth, including the unfolding of time. *Anō* time, then, is time under the sovereign sway of God, time that is God's faithful agent and instrument, subject in every respect to God's decrees and purposes.

Sometimes when we suffer, we can't see past our painful circumstances. God raises John to a new vantage point from which he can see the present in the light of the future. The next seventeen and a half chapters illuminate the events on earth as seen from heaven's perspective, walking us from the immediacy of John's day to *that* day: the return of Christ, the grand conclusion of human history, and the ushering in of the new heaven and the new earth.

Only then, only after the angel concludes his description of this sweep of events that "must soon take place" (Rev. 22:6), is John returned to his earthly vantage point. But now he is able to look upon the events of his day from God's perspective and to see—to his great encouragement—that the shambled chaos of daily events is in fact God-ordered and God-ordained. This may well be the primary theme of the book: the arrow of God-directed time is lancing unwaveringly toward the fulfillment of his redemptive purposes in human history in spite of humanity's mutiny and evil's seeming triumph.

Opposites Attract

If time as we experience it under the sun feels fleeting, wearying, meaningless, and devoid of God, time before the throne, as John glimpsed—and as we are invited to see with him—is just the opposite. It is replete with God, it marches inexorably toward the fulfillment of God's loving purposes for humanity, and, as a result, it encourages God's people.

Everlasting

Heavenward time is not fleeting but *everlasting*. We've seen that the Hebrew word *hebel* depicts the briefest of moments, devoid of meaning and disconnected from what transpires before and after. On the other end of the spectrum is the Hebrew word *olam*. It holds the idea of something in time or space that extends so far as to be lost from view, whether in the past, the future, or both. It is also used to speak of God and his work, which is *me'olam ad olam*, "from age to age" or "from everlasting to everlasting." The briefest puff compared to the broadest sweep of time—that is the difference between under-the-sun time and heavenward time.

In and of itself, time without end is no joyful prospect. We've all experienced circumstances when an abundance of time seems a curse rather than a gift. In his bleak *No Exit*, Jean-Paul Sartre envisions an eternity in which we are locked forever in a room with other fallen human beings endlessly sniveling and sniping at one another. What could be worse? In a sense, his image is accurate—at least for the one who comes to the end of this life without the hope of the Christian faith. Theologian Herman Bavinck captures this when he writes, "There is truth in the saying that in hell there is no eternity but only time."[2]

As I write this, my eldest son, who is engaged to be married this summer, is preparing to return to college for his final semester. He is counting these last days of vacation with dread, knowing he will have to leave behind his beautiful fiancée, with whom he has spent delightful but fleeting hours over the past three weeks. Again and again we hear him say, "I can't wait to get married!" He longs to stretch these snipped and stolen moments into an unbroken lifetime by the side of his beloved.

Time without end coupled with love without end is what gives us reason for joy. Twenty-six times Psalm 136 echoes with the refrain "his love endures forever." It is this prospect—not unending time but unending love—that truly makes heaven and the new creation so breathtakingly attractive.

In heavenward time, everything lasts. All that is good of this life, all that is of God, will be transformed by his gracious touch and persist forever (Rom. 8:28; 1 Cor. 3:10–13).

Purposeful

Heavenward time drips with loving purpose. According to the Bible, time conspires toward the fulfillment of God's ends. There will be a day "when the time of perfection [*teleios*] comes"(1 Cor. 13:10 NLT).

Paul elaborates on the goal of God's redemptive work in his letter to the church in Ephesus: "until we all reach unity in the faith and in the knowledge of the Son of God and become mature [*teleios*], attaining to the whole measure of the fullness of Christ" (4:13). The author of Hebrews identifies Jesus as the one who brings this about: "fixing our eyes on Jesus, the pioneer and perfecter [*teleiotes*] of faith" (12:2).

Teleios is a pivotal word in New Testament Greek. Translators have struggled to find just the right word for it in English. The NIV has "perfect," the NASB "complete," the ESV "mature," and the Amplified "full-grown." Each captures part of the word's nuanced meaning. What they all have in common is the idea that what was first intended has now come to pass. The original design has been completed; the plan is fulfilled.

Teleios captures the essential quality of heavenward time: it flies unerringly toward a particular end:

- God and humanity reconciled
- sin and evil eradicated
- creation redeemed
- the sons and daughters of God revealed
- God glorified

Whether or not we see it from our earthly vantage point, every minute of time carries us closer to the fulfillment of God's purposes.

This leads us to a final quality of heavenward time.

Replete with God

From where we sit here in under-the-sun time, God is, as far as our senses tell us, absent. Not so with heavenward time. It is replete with God. God towers over all, upstaging all else. We find him at the center, on the throne, ordering events, eliciting obedience, evoking praise. All hinges on his word and will. All obeys, time included. God is the falconer of time, which wings forth from his hand unerringly, intent to do his bidding.

Scripture affirms this again and again. For instance, through Isaiah God asserts his undisputed governance over the unfolding of time: "I foretold the former things long ago; my mouth announced them and I made them known; then suddenly I acted, and they came to pass" (Isa. 48:3). Paul expresses similar ideas. In Ephesians, he writes, "In him we were also chosen, having been predestined according to the plan of him who works out everything in conformity with the purpose of his will" (1:11). And in 1 Timothy 6:14–15, he speaks of "the appearing of our Lord Jesus Christ, which God will bring about in his own time."

In England, I visited the operations room at Duxford Airfield in which military leaders met to consider the progress of the Battle of Britain. A huge table stood in the middle of the room covered with a map of southern England, the Channel, and northern Europe. On the surface of the map, wooden blocks with small pennants marked the movements of the enemy and the identity, location, and size of the British squadrons that were in the air. These were regularly moved in response to reports wired in from observers' posts along the coast. Surrounding the table hung boards with information about the status of squadrons not yet airborne: planes, pilots, crews, and armament.

A raised gallery circling the table provided a comprehensive view of the action for the Allied squadron commanders. In response to what they saw before them, they sent out dispatches to the network of airports, ordering whatever was necessary to fulfill the commanders' plans.

The throne room of heaven is similar to that ops room, as God monitors the unfolding of events here on earth and marshals them to his ends. God is not only in charge of time; God is the central figure in the entire everlasting drama of redemption.

In the closing paragraphs of Scripture, in majestic words that herald the new reality to which all things move and in which all things have their end, a voice bellows, "God's dwelling place is now among the people, and he will dwell with them. They will be his people, and God himself will be with them and be their God." Then God assumes his seat upon the throne in the new creation, turns to John, and proclaims, "It is done. I am the Alpha and the Omega, the Beginning and the End" (Rev. 21:3, 6).

All of time leads unerringly to him, the Ancient of Days.

Eat, Drink, and Be Mindful

Time is a circle, and yet time is a line. We experience it as both. This brings us back, intriguingly, to the book of Ecclesiastes.

At first read, Ecclesiastes strikes us as the dreary diary of a disappointed old king. But don't be misled. Ecclesiastes is not devoid of hope or forward movement. Quite the opposite. I believe the Teacher wrote his painful dissection of under-the-sun life precisely so we would stop and consider whether there is something more.

As I read it, Ecclesiastes is the equivalent of C. S. Lewis's *Surprised by Joy* or G. K. Chesterton's *Orthodoxy*: a spiritual autobiography written to persuade others of the folly of life understood apart from God. With the same artful purposefulness we find in Lewis and Chesterton, the writer exposes the emptiness of daily life and the paucity of this-world answers before turning the eyes of his readers heavenward. In spite of being written three thousand years ago, Ecclesiastes speaks with remarkable contemporaneity to the heaven-rejecting, this-world spirit of our day.

"I have seen the burden God has laid on the human race," writes the author (Eccles. 3:10). The tedious cycling of days and nights gutted of meaning makes life nearly unbearable. But then he writes this: "He has made everything beautiful in its time. He has also set eternity in the human heart" (3:11). In spite of evidence to the contrary, we are not on a treadmill of time. "In its time" implies that God conspires with time, sequencing it and ordering it to his ends. In his hands, our today links to that day when all things will be set to rights, and our hearts echo with the knowledge of it.

"Yet no one can fathom what God has done from beginning to end," he continues (3:11). We *know* there is something more, but most of us cannot see it or, seeing it, cannot comprehend it. From earth's vantage point, there is no start or finish. Everything is a muddled middle. But it needn't be so. The key, according to Ecclesiastes, is for us to take our eyes off our cycling circumstances and set them on the Lord of our circumstances:

> Remember your Creator
>   in the days of your youth,
> before the days of trouble come. . . .
> Remember him—before the silver cord is severed . . .
>   and the spirit returns to God who gave it. (Eccles. 12:1,
>   6–7)

> Now all has been heard;
>   here is the conclusion of the matter:
> Fear God and keep his commandments,
>   for this is the whole duty of all mankind. (Eccles.
>   12:13)

If we do this, if we put our confidence in God, who orders time, we can walk through the hollow circling of this life with peace, joy, contentment, and purpose.

> Go, eat your food with gladness, and drink your wine with a joyful heart, for God has already approved what you do. Always be clothed in white, and always anoint your head with oil. Enjoy life with your wife, whom you love, all the days of this meaningless life that God has given you under the sun—all your meaningless days. (Eccles. 9:7–9)

Time is a circle; time is an arrow. We can experience it both ways. Like at O'Hare International Airport, life seems at one level to be nothing but endless circling about the airfield, but viewed at another, it is a single line of planes on final approach, vectored unerringly for the runway.

Dick and Sibyl Towner, my dear adoptive parents, had a 1920s home in Cincinnati graced with angles and gables. Of its many charming features I especially liked the attic door. I remember eyeing with intrigue that little knot of rope that hung from a small wooden panel in the middle of the upstairs hall. As I eventually learned, a light tug on the rope swung down a hinged door with a built-in wooden extension ladder. Instant access to the magical charms of that upper story.

The Bible calls us—commands us, actually—to climb regularly into the attic to seek a there-is-more-to-this-world vantage point. We pull down on that little knot of rope whenever we pray. We swing open the door whenever we open Scripture. Every time we worship, we climb up into the attic. Fellowship too opens the door and sets our feet on the rising steps.

Is this not the essence of hope: casting aside our certainty that this world and its events have the last word, laying hold of that knotted cord, and climbing into a heavenward perspective that sees God enthroned over this world?

Set your heart on things above.

8

The Vanishing Point

It seems our own impermanence is concealed from us. The trees stand firm, the houses we live in are still there. We alone flow past it all, an exchange of air.

Rainer Maria Rilke, "Second Duino Elegy"

Death is the destiny of everyone;
the living should take this to heart.

Ecclesiastes 7:2

Live as if you were to live forever; live as if you were to die tomorrow.

Algerian proverb

Depend upon it, sir, when a man knows he is to be hanged in a fortnight, it concentrates his mind wonderfully.

Samuel Johnson, *The Life of Samuel Johnson*

Are not my few days almost over?

Job 10:20

Could be today!

Steven Kaufman

In the last analysis, it is our conception of death which decides
our answers to all the questions that life puts to us.

Dag Hammarskjöld, *Markings*

The phrase "putting things in perspective" comes from the world of art. For centuries, up through the Middle Ages, artists wrestled to make their frescoes and paintings appear realistic. But no matter how hard they worked at it, they had trouble overcoming the sense that each part of the painting was disconnected and without relation to the other parts.

Stroll through the early and medieval section of a nearby art museum and this struggle will leap out at you. Figures in early works often seem flat and oddly placed. Instead of feeling anchored together in the composition, they are disproportionate and float like felt figures on a flannel board. Background buildings and cities have a similar piecemeal, two-dimensional quality.

Then came the Renaissance. In the early fifteenth century, architects in Florence such as Filippo Brunelleschi and Leon Battista Alberti began to capture perspective in their art. Drawing on insights found in Greek paintings made centuries earlier, they found a way of unifying a painting by adding an imaginary vanishing point on the horizon, a single *point of perspective* to which everything is related. Walls, steps, checkerboard floors, columned rows, and rooflines all are aligned to that point. Individual figures are arranged together to show perspective in a similar way: those nearer are larger, and those farther are smaller and placed behind the closer figures.

The entire painting suddenly comes together. Its subjects, once separate and disjointed, find their places in proportion to one another and in relationship to the things around them—all because everything in the painting is now related to a single fixed point on the horizon.

Memento Mori

As in art, so in life.

When we find a point of perspective, it lands us in our place, anchors us to the ground, fits together the various dislocated pieces of our lives and puts them all in right proportion to form a purposeful whole. We have just such a vanishing point: our coming death, the moment when our days on earth will end.

This is the second dimension of understanding the *kairos*: God calls us to be mindful not only of the end of the age but also of the end of our days. One hundred years from now, not one of us will be here. Either Christ will have come back, or our lives will have come to an end. For us, the effect is the same. Our earthly days are numbered.

When we live in conscious awareness that our days are numbered, things have a wonderful way of becoming clear.

On my recent hurried visit to London's National Gallery, I came upon a quirky work by Hans Holbein the Younger. Titled *The Ambassadors*, the painting is a portrait of two young dignitaries, both rising leaders, one in the courts, the other in the church. They stand stiffly by a desk on which are strewn symbols of their learning and accomplishments: books, globes, parchments, musical instruments, costly possessions. Across the bottom of the portrait, like a spill on the perfect checkered floor, is an odd splash of grays and blacks, not recognizable as anything in particular. A rug? A skin?

Painted in what is called anamorphic perspective, the spot suddenly comes into perfect focus for a viewer who stands below the painting and to the left—just where an unsuspecting houseguest would be as he walked up the stairs and, turning on the landing, glanced up at the painting. There, just inches above his head and looking straight at him, he would see a huge grinning skull.

In the mid-1300s, Europe was hit with a plague so severe that, in four years, one-third of the population—twenty million men, women, and children—died. For those who survived, their shared experience of the brevity and unpredictability of life led them to be much more mindful that each day was a gift.

In the wake of the plague, a new style of "moral art" developed that was designed to illuminate the preciousness of life. Known as *ars moriendi* ("the art of dying"), these paintings were riddled with symbolic reminders of the swift passing of time (an hourglass, oil lamp, or watch), the precariousness of life (wilted flowers, rotting or worm-eaten fruit, a swooping bird of prey, a scythe or sickle), and the finality of death (skulls, gates, cypress trees, the color black, ivy, and poppies). These symbols, called *memento mori* (literally, "remember you must die"), were often strategically placed amid the symbols of earthly success that so often surrounded the subject of a portrait.

Today, we focus exclusively on *ars vivendi* ("the art of living"), and death is placed on such a distant horizon that we often lose sight of it altogether. Yet when we live as though our days on earth will go on forever, nothing brings unity to the relationships we build or the work we do. After these people will come other people; after this work will come other work, ad infinitum. There's no particular connection between any one thing in my life and any other thing. Now this, now this, now this. We *spend* time; we don't invest it.

But if we live in the knowledge that our days on earth are finite and few (Ps. 39:4–5), that heaven awaits those who in this earthly life put the weight of their lives on Jesus Christ (John 3:16), and that in the meantime God has prepared acts of service in advance for us to do (Eph. 2:10), suddenly each relationship is vested with deeper meaning and each work with greater significance, and all of the pieces begin to cohere.

A clear vanishing point has a wonderful way of bringing things into perspective.

Numbering Our Days

I have a dear friend, a woman in our congregation, named Michele. Emaciated, bed-bound, bent by illness, unable to speak, she is one of the most beautiful women I know. Fifteen years ago, Michele was diagnosed with ALS (Lou Gehrig's disease), for which there is no known cure.

When, as a young wife and mother of two little children, she first learned of her diagnosis, she despaired. "What do I do now?" she asked her physical therapist. "Do you pray?" the therapist asked. Michele didn't, but she started. She began to seek God, and through a variety of means, God graciously drew her into the Christian faith.

Knowing that she is not likely to live long, and intent on the things that matter most, Michele lives with a focus and an urgency that elude most of us. Though she is confined all day to a recliner chair, has no use of her arms or legs, and has lost the ability to speak, she has found a number of creative avenues to tell what Jesus has done in her life. She created a website (www.meetmyfriend .com) on which she tells her story. While she still had limited use of one hand, she typed, with a mouse taped to her hand, one letter at a time. Now, having lost all use of her limbs, she uses motion-tracking software that allows her to type using her eyes.

Her best friend, Beth, and I were grinning as we talked recently about Michele's constant urging that we share our faith wherever we go. For example, once a week Beth runs errands for Michele, stopping at the grocery and other stores as needed. The first question from Michele when Beth gets back is always the same: "Did you talk with people about Jesus?" And when I preached a recent message that lacked a clear call to faith, she expressed her concern. She wants to make sure we've made the most of every moment and taken advantage of every opportunity.

In a newspaper article that shared her story with our community, her husband, Scott, reflected on the difference it has made to know that Michele's days are limited: "ALS has made us squeeze the most life out of each day. Our lives have never been more fulfilling. We don't have time to fuss and worry over the stuff we used to."[1]

The irony, of course, is that for all of us, not just for Michele, our days are numbered. Life on earth is a terminal illness for which there is no known cure.

The Never-Ending Story

Our world reinforces the myth of our immortality, sequestering any hint of impending death and perpetuating the myth that we will live forever.

Think, for instance, of the ads that bombard us. Apart from a few nagging commercials from those who wish us to invest in their retirement funds or buy their life insurance, the tide of commercial communication is away from acknowledging our coming death. Ads are filled with youthful actors and boundless opportunities.

And think of our experience of death via TV, the movies, and video games. Death has been removed from the real world and thrust back in our faces as entertainment. Death is the source of either excitement ("Run for your lives!") or amusement ("Blow him away!"), depending on whether the protagonist is the one doing the running or the one doing the killing. Death becomes something to penetrate our numbness and boredom at the end of a long day but certainly not something to be taken seriously.

We have so little exposure to real death. A hundred years ago, death was part of life. Higher infant and young-adult mortality rates meant few families were untouched by the loss of a brother, sister, son, or daughter. When someone died, visitation took place not in the awkwardly bland setting of a funeral "home," but in one's own, real home. The body was laid out in the front room for all to see. Death was found and felt in the midst of life. Not so today. The sick and dying are generally placed in hospitals and care facilities for the elderly where they can die tastefully, in discreet privacy. While hospice services are growing, they will always be the exception.

Doctors for the terminally ill can sometimes deny the approach of death, treating the illness but neglecting to care for the patient. When Sharon's father died of lymphoma a few years ago, he didn't even know he was dying. His doctors helped him in his denial, robbing him of the opportunity to prepare properly for his death and taking from his family the opportunity to say good-bye.

Little in our day-to-day life gives us occasion to mull on the transience of this life or the death that is to come—to our detriment. A sense of mortality adds urgency and brings clarity to the way we spend our precious time.

Seeing to the Other Side

When I was twenty, my parents died in a flying accident. Until that point, I had approached life as a boundless source of fun. I played, running from distraction to distraction. When my father's small plane went down in a storm in Virginia during finals of my sophomore year, I suddenly looked at life differently. For the first time, I asked what mattered, what was important.

I dropped out of my many empty amusements like adventure clubs and honor societies and began to get serious about life for the first time. I probed what mattered. Friends became more important, time fillers less. I became more interested in literature, philosophy, history. The pursuit of what mattered led me to questions of purpose, to spiritual things, ultimately to God, Jesus, surrender, and conversion.

Diane Ackerman tells of the practice of monks in Tibetan monasteries who, upon waking, lie on their beds with their eyes closed and think, "I'm going to die tonight. What shall I do with the rest of my time?" because, as she says, "It might be true of any day, and certainly will be true one day."[2]

When I turned forty, I decided to begin the day by reading portions of three related psalms. The experience was so powerful that I've reread them every time my birthday has rolled around since (which seems, for some reason, to be happening more frequently these days).

I begin with Psalm 139:

> You made all the delicate, inner parts of my body
> and knit me together in my mother's womb.
> Thank you for making me so wonderfully complex!
> Your workmanship is marvelous—and how well I
> know it.
> You watched me as I was being formed in utter seclusion,
> as I was woven together in the dark of the womb.
> You saw me before I was born.
> Every day of my life was recorded in your book.
> Every moment was laid out
> before a single day had passed. (vv. 13–16 NLT)

Then I read Psalm 39:

> Lord, remind me how brief my time on earth will be.
> Remind me that my days are numbered—
> how fleeting my life is.

> You have made my life no longer than the width of my
>   hand.
> My entire lifetime is just a moment to you;
>   at best, each of us is but a breath.
> We are merely moving shadows,
>   and all our busy rushing ends in nothing. (vv. 4–6 NLT)

My last stop is Psalm 90:

> You sweep people away like dreams that disappear.
>   They are like grass that springs up in the morning.
> In the morning it blooms and flourishes,
>   but by evening it is dry and withered. . . .
> Seventy years are given to us!
>   Some even live to eighty.
> But even the best years are filled with pain and trouble;
>   soon they disappear, and we fly away. . . .
> Teach us to realize the brevity of life,
>   so that we may grow in wisdom. (vv. 5–6, 10, 12 NLT)

Talk about perspective.

When we're mindful that our days are numbered, we live differently. We're more likely to recognize the difference between the important and the unimportant and to let the unimportant things go. We're less likely to fritter away our dwindling days on lesser things. Relationships will matter more, things less. The spiritual will rise in importance, the material will fall. Urgency will mark our pursuit of those things that matter most; indifference will mark our pursuit of lesser things. And each new day will have about it a blanket of gratitude: here is another gift—and yet another, and another still—of which we are undeserving but joyful beneficiaries.

An awareness that our days are limited imbues them with both a steward's sense of urgency (now rather than later) and a strategist's sense of clarity (this rather than that).

If Not Now, When?

Years ago, I hiked to the top of Mount Oxford, a fourteen-thousand-foot peak in the Colorado Rockies, with two of my closest friends. Not long before, I had presided at the funeral of a woman who died in her fifties. I had been deeply moved by the way she was remembered by those who gathered to celebrate her resurrection and to honor her life.

As we began the hike, I put some questions before us: What would you like your friends and family members to say about you at your memorial service? What do you want to be remembered for? What will your obituary say? What, in other words, is a life well lived?

We talked about what mattered most to us: family, ministry, friends, our various interests. Inevitably, the topic led us past those things on *our* hearts and caused us to ask what was most on the heart of God. By what qualities would he have us be known?

We spent most of the ascent talking about it. Somewhere around twelve thousand feet, I arrived at my answer. I wanted to be remembered as someone who was open to whatever God wanted to do *in* me and faithful to whatever God wanted to do *through* me. If that were true of me, then the things most on God's heart would be first on my own, and the things I did would be the things God wanted done. What more could matter?

"Resolved," wrote Jonathan Edwards, "never to do anything which I would be afraid to do if it were the last hour of my life."[3] Or, as I once put it in my journal in a much more down-to-earth way, "I don't want to waste my time piddling around doing anything less than what God made me to do."

Keeping in mind that our world—and we ourselves—will end is crucial to understanding the times. Time is short.

Equally crucial is calling to mind God's claim upon our time. Time is not ours. That's where we turn next.

9

Whose Time Is It?

This is my time.

Usain Bolt

If I could have my time. If I could have my time again and live those days over. Then nothing of this. I would have allowed nothing of it to pass neither one hour nor one minute. If I had known the time were so soon fled I would have had more of it I would have taken more. I feel it has been stolen from me and it seems like a terrible injustice.

Peter Hobbs, *The Short Day Dying*

We try, when we wake, to lay the new day at God's feet; before we have finished shaving, it becomes *our* day and God's share in it is felt as a tribute which we must pay out of "our own" pocket, a deduction from the time which ought, we feel, to be "our own."

C. S. Lewis, *The Problem of Pain*

No hurry; I can wait. I have this morning's paper here. Your time shall be mine.

Mr. Perker to Mr. Pickwick, Charles Dickens,
The Posthumous Papers of the Pickwick Club

> Your life belongs to God. You're not sharing your time and talents with Him; He is sharing His with you!
>
> Greg Laurie, *Let God Change Your Life*

> Let me not be at my own disposal.
>
> Puritan prayer, *The Valley of Vision*

A light drizzle fell on the windshield as I pulled out of the parking lot.

We were trying to squeeze in a family dinner between my work commitments, my daughter's friend time, and my son's soccer practice. As sometimes happens, we were shy a few ingredients, so I had made a hurried run to the grocery store on my way home from work, painfully aware of how close we were cutting the time.

Easing into traffic from the store, I caught sight of an older man walking slowly along the slick sidewalk. His eyes were twisted into an anxious squint, and a plastic grocery bag dangled at his wrist as he tried to wipe the mist from his glasses. His drooped shoulders were darkened with rain.

In the half second after I passed him, I realized I knew him. He was a new member of our congregation. In the next half second after that, I calculated that it would take me no more than ten minutes to turn around, pick him up, and deliver him to his doorstep.

But I didn't. No time. I drove right past him, another victim of the press of other things. My time demands trumped his. Lord, have mercy.

Mine?

I love maps. Part of the fun of them is how they expose the way we think about life and the world around us. *Centrality* is the word cartographers use to describe what occupies the prominent spot

at the center of a map. Almost invariably, maps are self-centered—
ethnocentric is the mapmaker term.

You see it in ancient Chinese maps, ancient Mesoamerican maps,
medieval European maps, Victorian British maps. But they aren't
the only culprits. Until quite recently, American-made world maps
plunked the United States squarely in the middle, even though it
meant whacking the great landmass of Asia in half. When I was a
teenager the *New Yorker* came out with a cover by Saul Steinburg
that came to be called "A New Yorker's View of the World." Down-
town Manhattan covers most of the page. The rest of the United
States is no more than a big square field on the other side of the
Hudson River, littered with a few random rocks and a couple of
city names—Kansas City, Las Vegas, Los Angeles. Beyond stretches
the Pacific, about the width of the Hudson, on the other side
of which lie three thin bands labeled China, Japan, and Russia.
Inevitably, mapmakers place themselves in the center. The same
is true about the way we occupy time. "David Henderson's view
of time" is dominated by me. I am time's center, time's reference
point. I take up two-thirds of the page.

Time is my possession. It's mine. All mine. I begin the day with
a finite lump of it, and it is mine to dole out to the projects and
responsibilities, the people and pursuits that come to me over the
course of the day.

I scoop out some for my quiet time, some more for breakfast
and the morning paper, a chunk for my commute, a big swath of
it for work, and so on until I've scraped out the last of it by the
end of the day. Others may take from it, cut into it, demand some
of it, but it belongs to me. It's mine.

But is that how God would have us view the hours and days
spread out before us? C. S. Lewis suggests otherwise. In his devi-
ous *Screwtape Letters*, Lewis imagines how a senior demon might
advise a fellow fiend in his efforts to undermine God's work in a
believer's life. Among his suggestions are these related to time:

Now you will have noticed that nothing throws him into a passion so easily as to find a tract of time which he reckoned on having at his own disposal unexpectedly taken from him. It is the unexpected visitor (when he looked forward to a quiet evening), or a friend's talkative wife (turning up when he looked forward to a *tete-a-tete* with the friend), that throws him out of gear. Now he is not yet so uncharitable or slothful that these small demands on his courtesy are *in themselves* too much for it. They anger him because he regards his time as his own and feels it has been stolen.

You must therefore zealously guard in his mind the curious assumption "My time is my own." Let him have the feeling that he starts each day as the lawful possessor of twenty-four hours. Let him feel as a grievous tax that portion of this property which he has to make over to his employers, and as a generous donation that further portion which he allows to religious duties. But what he must never be permitted to doubt is that the total from which these deductions have been made was, in some mysterious sense, his own personal birthright.[1]

The notion that my *time* is mine can only stand as long as I believe that *I* am mine, that my life is beholden to no one but me.

Yours?

When Jesus comes into the picture, our perspective begins to change. He turns us outward from a life lived for self and, for the first time, begins to make us genuinely mindful of the needs of others.

For example, before what he called "the Great Change" in his life, William Wilberforce spent much of his time on what he later called frivolities: dances, theater, parties, and other empty social events. But after his conversion to Christianity, his view of time changed dramatically. Realizing that his time was no longer his own, he wrote this resolution in his diary: "To endeavor from this moment to amend my plan for time. I hope to live more than heretofore to God's glory and my fellow-creature's good."[2]

Giving heed to Jesus's call to love our neighbor as ourselves, we shift from thinking of time as *mine* to time as *yours*. Isn't this, after all, what Jesus was saying when he told the story of the good Samaritan (Luke 10:25–37): that our time is not our own but belongs instead to the person in our life who has needs? The Levite and the priest saw their time as their own and, with windshield wipers flapping and clock ticking, drove right past. But it is the Samaritan, laying aside his own claims on his time to tend to the needs of another, whom Jesus calls us to emulate.

Jesus himself certainly seemed to live by the my-time-is-yours principle. For example, Mark recounts the time when a weary Jesus and his disciples tried to duck away for some much-needed replenishment and time together. "Because so many people were coming and going that they did not even have a chance to eat, he said to them, 'Come with me by yourselves to a quiet place and get some rest.' So they went away by themselves in a boat to a solitary place" (6:31–32).

But the crowds ran ahead and were waiting on the shoreline when Jesus landed. His response? "He had compassion on them, because they were like sheep without a shepherd" (v. 34). So, as Mark goes on to relate, he gathered them together, taught them about the kingdom, and fed them a feast. This seems to indicate that another person's need always determines what we should do with our time. Or does it?

His?

Looking closer at Jesus's example, we see a still more radical way of thinking about our time. For instance, in Luke's Gospel, we're told of a time when crowds of people from all over the region brought to Jesus their sick and demon-possessed. Jesus healed some of them but by no means all. Then he ducked away to a solitary place. When the people finally found him, he prepared to leave again. When they tried to keep him from leaving, he said, "I must proclaim the good news of the kingdom of God to the other towns also, because that is why I was sent" (Luke 4:43). Jesus turned away from needs that stood before him. How do we understand this?

The more nuanced picture that emerges is that Jesus viewed his time neither as his nor as belonging to those who surrounded him and presented him with their needs. Jesus understood that his time belonged to the Father, and he spent his time doing those things to which the Father *called* him—whether spending time alone, focusing on his disciples, or ministering to the crowds. "I have come down from heaven," he insisted, "not to do my will but to do the will of him who sent me" (John 6:38). And earlier, "The Son can do nothing by himself; he can only do what he sees his Father doing, because whatever the Father does the Son also does" (John 5:19).

Jesus's ministry presses us past the simple (but overwhelming) idea that need constitutes call. Another step is required in our understanding.

> If my time is my time, I do whatever I want.
>
> If my time is your time, I do whatever you need.
>
> But if my time belongs to God, I do whatever he calls me to.

I remember painfully my bunk bed at Culver Woodcraft Camp. The bedsprings had probably been crafted before Columbus discovered the New World. As a result, the bed sagged something fierce. I always tried to fall asleep on the outer edges of the mattress, but no matter how hard I tried, within a few hours I'd wind up balled up in the hot, low-lying center.

Our universal reflex as fallen human beings is to roll into the center of the bed, to see all things as revolving around us. We do this with our relationships (about me), our possessions (for me), and our time (my own).

What is a kingdom solution to the problem of busyness? The answer is both profoundly simple and profoundly challenging. A kingdom requires but two things: a king and a loyal subject whose life and fealty belong to the king. The kingdom solution? Let the king decide how the subject spends his time.

In *Amish Grace*, their study of the Amish response to the tragic shooting of ten of their schoolgirls, Donald Kraybill and his fellow writers introduce a word that stands at the center of Amish life: *Gelassenheit*. English translations of the word include "composure," "calm," and "tranquility." It is a core virtue they seek to embody as Christian believers.[3]

Behind this word is a prerequisite posture of the heart toward God: submission. The Amish word for this is *Uffgevva* ("give up"). It is captured in the favorite prayer of the Amish: "Thy will be done" (Matt. 6:10 KJV). According to one Amish believer, "*Uffgevva* means giving up self and accepting God's will. That's what our life is all about. It's the biggest thing about being Amish."[4] Another explained, "It's a yieldedness to whatever God sends. . . . We don't pray for rain. We wait for rain, and when it comes, we thank God for it."[5]

Ultimately, the way we view the time before us is connected to the way we view ourselves before God. Jesus put the matter plainly: "Those of you who do not give up everything you have cannot be my disciples" (Luke 14:33). To which a loyal subject answers, in the words of Jeremiah, "LORD, I know that people's lives are not their own; it is not for them to direct their steps" (10:23).

While no passage in the Bible spells it out, the clear implication of verses such as Psalm 90:12 ("Teach us to number our days"), Jeremiah 10:23 ("People's lives are not their own"), and

1 Corinthians 6:19 ("You are not your own") is that our time is not our time after all. It belongs to another.

Collision Course

A couple of years ago, the elders of my church graciously granted me eight weeks for renewal leave. I committed to spend half the time writing and the other half—oh, the things I was going to do! Take piano lessons, do some watercolor painting, take an architectural boat tour in Chicago, head away for a four- or five-day retreat. I still remember breathlessly reading through my list with Sharon, oblivious to (or, more honestly, choosing to ignore) the weariness on her face.

The time came, and I got started. But just a week in, in the course of my writing, I "happened" to reread Deuteronomy 5 and its provisions of the Sabbath. I noticed for the first time how the passage addresses the need for rest for the *whole* family and not just one individual. "You shall not do any work, neither you, nor your son or daughter, nor your male or female servant . . . so that [they] may rest, as you do" (v. 14). The heart of God is that my whole household should be replenished, not just me.

Struck by my selfishness in crafting the entire renewal leave with thought only of myself, I opened my fists and let all those self-serving dreams of mine slide through my relaxed fingers. I now saw clearly that they weren't God's idea of how my time should be spent at all. One of the most enduring pictures from those (revised) eight weeks is of my wife and me sitting on our deck, side by side, beginning each day by leisurely enjoying time with the Lord and each other.

It is one of the most radical and freeing notions there is: my time does not belong to me. But for those of us bent upon the efficient use of "our" time, swinging around to that new way of thinking can be confoundedly difficult.

Dietrich Bonhoeffer experienced the messy complexity of life in community with his seminary students. His book *Life Together* anticipates the collision between the way we reflexively view time as our own and the way God would have us view our time as his.

> We must allow ourselves to be interrupted by God. God will be constantly crossing our paths and canceling our plans by sending us people with claims and petitions. We may pass them by, preoccupied with our more important tasks. . . . When we do that we pass by the visible sign of the Cross raised athwart our path to show us that, not our way, but God's way must be done. It is a strange fact that Christians and even ministers frequently consider their work so important and urgent that they will allow nothing to disturb them. They think they are doing God a service in this, but actually they are disdaining God's "crooked yet straight path" (Gottfried Arnold). They do not want a life that is crossed and balked. But it is part of the discipline of humility that we must not spare our hand where it can perform a service and that we do not assume that our schedule is our own to manage, but allow it to be arranged by God.[6]

Wasting Our Lives

When we surrender our time to God, we sometimes discover that he values different things than we do.

Sharon and I had been to dinner with friends. When we walked out of the restaurant late in the evening, a man approached us and asked for some money. What followed might have been a source of great amusement to the man were he not so hungry and tired.

First, the four of us pulled aside and talked about our options. We agreed that it would be best not simply to hand him some cash, because we couldn't be sure he would make good use of it. If we did anything at all, it should be in the form of food or gas or whatever he most needed. We then realized we didn't know what his real needs were.

So we went back and talked to him some more. He patiently explained that he just wanted something to eat. Then we pulled aside again, trying to figure out what we could do. We knew it would be best if one of us spent some time with him to try to have that personal touch and in some way incarnate the gospel. But it was late, the nearest fast-food restaurant was several blocks away, and we had all come in one car. So if one of us stayed, it would delay the rest of us. And it was getting late for the sitters, and . . .

After talking among ourselves for at least ten minutes, we told him we were sorry but we couldn't help him, and we walked away. Looking back, I think how much better it would have been if we had just smiled, handed him a ten, told him that God was crazy about him and saw him in his need, and told him to go treat himself to a meal. In other words, if we had "wasted" money on him.

I need to learn the same lesson with my time. I need to be more willing to "waste" it on things that matter to God more than they matter to me.

I'm not advocating diminishing the value of time or throwing time away but rather *raising* its value by seeing it through the eyes of others and under the sway of God. That will mean prying open the fist a bit and giving God room to move, becoming less bent on calculating my responsible use of it down to the minute and more willing to "waste" it on the people God has placed around me.

Squatters are those who, having loitered long enough in a certain place, begin to feel entitled to it. We are time squatters, every one of us. Time doesn't belong to us. But we've lived so long at time's center that we feel as though it does. God calls us to become displaced persons, to pack our bags and move out of Time Square, which we've so long and so smugly occupied.

Prime Meridian

Medieval cartographers lacked detailed geographical knowledge, but they knew who was—and who was not—at the center of the world. They drew world maps known today as T and O maps. A circle of water around the perimeter, representing the oceans, formed the O, and a T-shaped Mediterranean divided the land into the three known continents: Europe, Asia, and Africa. Quite purposefully, oriented as they were with east at the top, these *mappa mundi* formed the distinctive shape of a cross.

This is the sort of cartography by which God calls us to orient our lives. The cross—symbol of a life laid down, a life wasted for others—should define the terrain on which we walk and live, for not just we but all things are his, redeemed on a crossbeam. The true prime meridian—the point of reference that rightly orients all of the space/time world—is drawn right through its center.

—

There really are only two ways to view our time. We can follow the culture into a *driven* life, in which we view our time as our own, to meet our own needs. Or we can follow Christ into a *called* life, in which we yield up our time, giving it back to its rightful owner, and then allow him to lead us into the life he has already designed for us.[7]

I choose the one that includes time to pick up a man in the rain.

But before we turn there, we must consider one other dimension of understanding the times.

10

A Single Eye

Cover of a birthday card: The occasion of your birthday is a propitious time to put aside material things and get in touch with the spiritual here and now. Understand that there is no past; there is no future.

Inside: There is no present.

How rare it is for a man to be contemporary with himself. Most persons, in feeling, in imagination, in purpose, in resolution, in wish, in longing, are a hundred thousand miles in advance of themselves.

Søren Kierkegaard, *Christian Discourses*

We are very distractible people in a very distracting world.

Leighton Ford, *The Attentive Life*

Begin each day to live, and count each separate day as a separate life.

Seneca, *Moral Letters to Lucilius*

"What day is it?" asked Winnie the Pooh.
"It's today," squeaked Piglet.
"My favorite day," said Pooh.

A. A. Milne, *Winnie the Pooh*

I was crossing Vineyard Sound on a ferry. I could still see, gray on the horizon far behind, the contour of Martha's Vineyard. The sky was clear and so was the view of the heath, the beaches, and the trim white cottages. I turned, facing into the wind, and squinted, my eyes watering. Far ahead, the water dissolved imperceptibly into haze, obscuring the coastline of Cape Cod, where we would eventually land.

I was in the middle of a seven-mile-wide body of water on a small, bobbing ferry, churning through the swells, the air acrid with diesel smoke and fishy brine.

Suppose someone standing next to me had asked, "Where are we right now?" How might I have answered? Spread my arms out and said, "In this sound"? Or pointed straight down and said, "On this boat"?

From Time to Time

It is a strange and misleading thing, the ocean-like expanse of time around us, not unlike that spread of sea at the Cape. As ones whose memory and imagination can throw us far forward and far backward, when is *now*?

From whatever our location in time, we can see far behind and well ahead. My earliest childhood memories are of looking at the light of the sun playing on the walls of my room when I was less than two. I also remember flipping upside down into the snow while on a disk that my dad spun around on a rope in our backyard, playing in our rock garden, and walking with my mom down the hill to the train station near our house, all memories from when I was just two or three. From those moments to the present, half a century later, hundreds of thousands of remembered events flesh out and fill in the past.

This is also largely true of the future. When I look ahead, I project my continued life, thoughts, family, friends, home, work into the future and—whether accurate or not—easily envision something of what the coming months and even years may hold.

But my sweeping island-to-cape sense of the here and now is misleading, for my life is lived not in the vast sweep of the oceanic past and future but on the small couple-hundred-square-foot bobbing moment that we call the present. It is only in the now that I can do anything: think, feel, decide, act, listen, speak, love, live. "Only in the present," says Jorge Luis Borges, "do things happen."[1]

That doesn't mean that only the present matters. I just spoke with friends whose mother, stricken with dementia, has lost a sense of how past events inform the present and of how her present choices will affect her future. She can't remember the doctor's admonition an hour earlier that she should eat now, and she can't connect her decisions about eating her yogurt and pudding now with the possibility of getting stronger and going home from the hospital sooner. She is trapped in the present.

As followers of Christ, how should we understand our relationship to past, present, and future? Let's consider future and past first, then turn to the present.

All That Is to Come

Dag Hammarskjöld wrote, "For all that is past—thanks. For all that is to come—yes."[2] His words capture beautifully a biblical posture toward past and future.

Each of us has a bent toward either the past or the future. For me, the expanse of ocean up ahead is the lure. I love standing on the prow and trying to make out what lies shrouded in the fog ahead.

In earlier seasons of my ministry, I sometimes engaged in what you might call "fishful thinking," a combination of wishful thinking and fishing for other options. Calls came every so often about other positions. Some were attractive because I imagined them as opportunities free of all difficulty: no opposition or misunderstandings or unreasonable expectations. Others were appealing because I imagined them to be a better expression of my gifts. What if I became a college chaplain? What if I got my PhD and taught at a seminary? What if I became a full-time teaching pastor at another church? What if I pastored overseas? What if I became a full-time writer? Reasonable possibilities, perhaps. What is unreasonable is the amount of time I spent outside of the present mulling the options and imagining myself elsewhere, doing something other than what I had been called to do right then, right there.

Several years ago, when I shared some of these musings about God's call on my life with a good friend, he encouraged me to set them aside for a season and be present to what was before me. If God wanted to raise them up again, he easily could. My friend understood what I didn't yet see, that my wishful imaginings—which I liked to think of as being open to the will of God—could as often be a heart of rebellion or discontent or selfishness in disguise, a way of being closed to the will of God and living in a preferred elsewhere.

Jesus cautions against living around the corner into what has not yet happened: "Do not worry about tomorrow, for tomorrow will worry about itself. Each day has trouble enough of its own" (Matt. 6:34). We live toward the future, not in it.

Shouldn't we be concerned about using our gifts to their full? Well, yes. Wouldn't it be best if we were in a place where we felt respected and loved? It might be. Wouldn't it be great if we served where our every idea came to be? Perhaps. But God doesn't always call us to places where our every gift will find its full expression right now or where our days are full of unbroken delight. Sometimes we are called to do things we don't want to do and aren't good at so God can teach us to rely on him instead of our abilities and so others can step forward with their gifts. Sometimes God calls us to things that are just plain hard and to settings that are outright painful so he can refine and prune us and use us, stripping from us the parts that don't resemble the Jesus we love. Eyes repeatedly wandering to the future only add to the pain while limiting our ability to receive the riches and purposes God has for us in the present.

All That Is Past

While some are more prone to lean out into the future, the bent of others is toward strolling repeatedly the corridors of the past. They rethink conversations they've had, classes they've taught, purchases they've made, decisions they've arrived at, interactions they've had, comments others have made.

Revisiting the past is a natural reflex, expressive of our longing to undo what is done, to put things to right. If only I could have made a different choice. If only that could have come out differently. Other memories are of a fonder sort, and we can easily drift back into their gentle joys, particularly when things aren't going so well right now. Either way, we allow the past to creep back into the present and become the present all over again, robbing us of life now, in this moment.

Speaking of the ongoing transformative work of God, who is conforming him in death and in life to Christ, Paul cautions, "Not that I have already obtained all this, or have already arrived at my goal, but I press on to take hold of that for which Christ Jesus took hold of me. Brothers and sisters, I do not consider myself yet to have taken hold of it. But one thing I do: Forgetting what is behind and straining toward what is ahead, I press on toward the goal to win the prize for which God has called me heavenward in Christ Jesus" (Phil. 3:12–14). We live from the past, not in it.

Years ago, in a rare and quirky event, a migraine caused traces of permanent damage to the occipital region of my brain, which is one of the areas that process vision. Called *palinopsia*, which means "seeing again," this affliction impacts the cortical inhibitors that rid us continually of old visual images so we can pay attention to the new ones that are ever streaming in. As a result, in my vision the past lingers in the present for a split second, causing strange visual effects and sometimes posing interesting challenges when it comes to reading.

We are all afflicted with spiritual palinopsia at times, a proneness to allow the past to linger in the present and cloud our ability to see things as they are. Of this ailment God means to heal us.

"I will repay you for the years the locusts have eaten," promises the Lord through Joel (2:25). We can't live in the past, and we can't change it, but we can stake our confidence on God's promise that he will redeem the past.

Now and Then

God's redemption assures us of an inheritance and a dowry. Think of the treasures stored in these twin chests:

The past contains	The future holds
life given	uncertainties answered
life redeemed	hope fulfilled
failures forgiven	brokenness repaired
faithfulness experienced	promises kept
mercies new every morning	all things made new

No other worldview answers our concerns about the past and the future as Christianity does. God has the last word over both, giving us the freedom to live fully present to him in the present.

The longer I am in Christ, the more I can trace the wise ways of God in ordering my life—past, present, and future. These particular relationships (whether joyful or challenging), these particular circumstances (whether easy or difficult), these particular turns of the road (whether to my liking or not), all passing through God's fingers and threaded through the narrow needle that is my life: in the midst of them, we pilgrims may wonder at the hidden ways of God. Only as we gain a promontory along the road and look back do we begin to see his loving designs in all things. The promise of Romans 8:28—"we know that in all things God works for the good of those who love him"—is borne out again and again. Time always proves the wisdom of God.

Centuries ago, Francis de Sales wrote, "The past must be abandoned to God's mercy . . . the future to divine Providence."[3] It is not our view of time and its passing but our view of God and his working that allows us to live with gratitude for the past and with expectancy for the future. Thanks, and yes.

Here and Now

We look back with thankfulness and we look ahead with anticipation, but we live in the present, because there God meets us and we him.

Scripture singles out the present moment ("now," "today") as the time we encounter God and are urged to respond to him. Today, we bring our needs to him; today, we receive his gifts; today, we express our thanks. Two familiar passages press us into a moment-by-moment posture of dependency and gratitude.

> The LORD said to Moses, ". . . In the morning you will be filled with bread. Then you will know that I am the LORD your God." . . . In the morning there was a layer of dew around the camp. When the dew was gone, thin flakes like frost on the ground appeared on the desert floor. When the Israelites saw it, they said to each other, "What is it?" . . . Moses said to them, "It is the bread the LORD has given you to eat. This is what the LORD has commanded: 'Everyone is to gather as much as they need.' . . . No one is to keep any of it

until morning." . . . Each morning everyone gathered as much as they needed. (Exod. 16:11–16, 19, 21)

Give us today our daily bread. (Matt. 6:11)

Now is when we experience God and his provision. Now is also the moment to decide and act.

See, I set before you *today* life and prosperity, death and destruction. . . . *This day* I call the heavens and the earth as witnesses against you that I have set before you life and death, blessings and curses. *Now* choose life, so that you and your children may live and that you may love the LORD your God, listen to his voice, and hold fast to him. (Deut. 30:15, 19–20, italics added)

As God's co-workers we urge you not to receive God's grace in vain. For he says,

"In the time of my favor I heard you,
    and in the day of salvation I helped you."

I tell you, *now* is the time of God's favor, *now* is the day of salvation. (2 Cor. 6:1–2, italics added)

Now is when we turn. Now is when we resolve. Now is when we decide. Now is when we live.
Other examples abound:

Today, if only you will hear his voice,
    "Do not harden your hearts." (Ps. 95:7–8)

Go now and leave your life of sin. (John 8:11)

Now that you know these things, you will be blessed if you do them. (John 13:17)

Now finish the work, so that your eager willingness to do it may be matched by your completion of it. (2 Cor. 8:11)

We instructed you how to live in order to please God, as in fact you are living. Now we ask you and urge you in the Lord Jesus to do this more and more. (1 Thess. 4:1)

See to it, brothers and sisters, that none of you has a sinful, unbelieving heart that turns away from the living God. But encourage one another daily, as long as it is called "Today," so that none of you may be hardened by sin's deceitfulness. (Heb. 3:12–13)

We are tempted all the time to step out of the present moment and to turn toward the past or the future. But God would have us take with us what is beneficial from the past without allowing its memories or regrets to keep pushing into the present and robbing us of life today. And we are called to open ourselves and ready ourselves for the gifts to come in the days ahead without allowing our preparing and planning and dreaming to cut into life lived in the now.

Attending the Present

Living in the present requires that we give ourselves to one thing only—the one thing that is before us. But our world clamors to divide our gaze; it seduces us into attending to a choir of sirens that sing all around us.

- As we drive: the road, the music on our iPod, that billboard, the passenger next to us, the unfinished conversation with our spouse
- When we have friends over: the person next to us, the person across the room, the phone in our pocket, the game that's on TV, the list of things to do that is running through our head
- While we do our homework: the physics in front of us, the episode of *24* that's on, our brother who's talking, the show that's on the other channel that we don't want to miss

- As we listen to a sermon: the message, the announcements in the bulletin, the twisted collar of the man in front of us, the child babbling three rows up, the bored choir member over the pastor's shoulder, the people we need to catch as soon as the service is over

A friend gave me a big grin and asked, "How was your weekend?" As I began to answer, he looked down at his cell phone and started to read a text. When he looked back up, his face was blank, like he'd woken up in the middle of our conversation and wondered how he'd gotten there. He hadn't heard a word I'd said. Attention is a sweet gift, all the more sweet for its increasing rarity in our culture.

A *Fox Trot* comic shows Andy sitting next to her husband, both of them staring straight ahead. She muses, "Ever feel like life is just zipping by? That the clock is ticking and there's no turning it back? That every second that passes is a precious second you'll never see again?" Roger turns to her and says, "I'm sorry, could you repeat that? I was watching the beer commercial."[4]

It's rare these days to meet someone who knows how to sustain focus on one person: to show interest, ask good questions, listen carefully, and follow up with more questions. Attention—a single gaze—is what the present requires but rarely fully gets, according to Maggie Jackson in *Distracted*, her exploration of our culture's attention deficit disorder. Alan Wallace, a fellow participant with Jackson on a mountain retreat, commented:

> If a person leaps in and sacrifices his life—you leap in and save a baby and then you die—you've given your whole life in one piece. That's a wonderful sacrifice. Greater love hath no man than he who lays down his life for another. Jesus, right? So that's pretty good. But when we give another person our attention, we're giving away that *portion* of our life. We don't get it back. We're giving

our attention to what seems worthy of our life from moment to moment. Attention, the cultivation of attention, is absolutely core.[5]

Jesus says, "If your eye is single, your whole body will be full of light" (Matt. 6:22, author's trans.). The idea is of looking at someone else without any view to ourselves or what is best for us. While in the context Jesus is speaking of material greed, his words are every bit as apt for time greed. When we clamor hungrily to attend to more than one thing, we are thinking of ourselves, not of the one before us.

"Love is focused attention," Leighton Ford writes.[6] It requires of us that we learn the rigorous art of narrowing our gaze. "The art of being wise," according to William James, "is the art of knowing what to overlook."[7]

Focal Point

God has endowed us with the capacity to imagine and dream and reflect and plan without regard to time. We can remember back and think ahead. This topples us—constantly—out of the now, spilling us over into the no-longer and the not-yet. It's one way we are distinct from the animal realm and mirror the God in whose image we have been created.

But, utterly unlike God and exactly like the rest of creation, we are caught in the sluice of time, living life one—and only one— moment at a time. Our lives are time-bound, squeezed through the keyhole of the present. What might it look like to embrace this aspect of our creatureliness rather than to rail against it? To see the narrowing of our focus as a gift?

Think of a tube of cake frosting. The very tininess of that hole at the end of the tube is what allows the cake decorator to fashion a work of art with the blob of frosting that lies behind it, as opposed to simply slathering the cake with coating. Think of a firefighter, who with precision plays a lake of water on the source of a fire. Or of a saxophone player, who gathers a portion of earth's atmosphere into his lungs and then directs a stream of air into a narrow hole from the other end of which spills melody.

Think of an artist like my daughter who has a palette with a dozen colors but holds only one brush and applies paint but one stroke at a time. By contrast, have you seen what happens when a child grabs three or four crayons in each hand and scrawls two-fisted across a piece of paper (or the family room wall)?

Art and life are born of narrowing, of restriction. A narrowing to one thing is what lets me be deliberate in a decision, or productive in a project, or attentive to a person. To this one thing, to this one person, I give myself.

The times I feel most unproductive, when my wheels most spin like bald tires on a patch of ice, are precisely those moments when I refuse to submit to the narrowing funnel of time and I try to attend to more than one thing at one time. I remember going to a friend's cabin for a retreat with my wife. After we finally got settled in, I plunked down by the fire with a stack of seven books: a couple of science books, a fiction classic, a history book, a biography, a play, and a sociology book. I picked one up, read a paragraph or two, then put it down and started another, then dropped it and grabbed another, all the way through the pile. It was silly; I was trying to read them all at the same time. Eventually, I slowed down, picked up the one that held my attention, and put the rest away.

Only living within the bounds of time—one thing at one time—allows me to enter freely and fully into the moment: to delight in a novel with abandon, to trace the face of a loved one without hurry, to leisurely walk the corridors of a conversation, to study the color pattern of an unfamiliar bird, to doggedly pursue the completion of an idea.

In the face of our unmannerly impulse to try to jam a moment with a dozen competing tasks, God calls us to a civility of the interior, to learn how to stand at the door of the present and say, "Please, after you."

An unexpected feature of the roads I traveled in Ireland was the regular appearance of large road signs placed just outside of towns and villages that read, "Traffic Calming." At first, I had no idea what they were heralding, but I began to make the connection.

The roads I traveled from town to town were two-lane highways with wide shoulders. As in the United States, it is common for cars to pass, crossing over the center line and moving out into the oncoming lane. And in Ireland, it is common for slower vehicles to drive on the shoulder and let the quicker cars use the main lane. As they descend upon a sleepy little village like Knocknagashel, with narrow streets and ambling pedestrians, cars can be zipping along in any of three lanes.

Hence the Traffic Calming device. First, you come upon a jarring series of zebra-striped triangles painted on both sides of the highway. That leads to a wedge of raised concrete on each side of the primary lane, like a narrowing pinball slot, on top of which are mounted bright lights, an angled arrow pointing to the severely narrowed gap, and a speed limit sign that slows traffic to, say, 40 kilometers per hour. All this conspires to gather cars into a single, slow, safe lane of traffic. No passing. No speeding. No doubling up in the lanes. One at a time.

As I careened along the roads of Ireland, I started imagining signs staked along the roads of my life announcing, "Life Calming." Slow down, stay in the present, give yourself to one thing at a time, all to the glory of God.

God means for us to understand the times, to be intimately acquainted with the watery deep, to know its shoals and shorelines. Between the commencement of God's redemptive work and its conclusion, between the first coming of Christ and his return, between our first breath and our last, between the receding past and the approaching future, this is the patch of water we are given to sail.

But on what heading, and under what sail? To that we turn next, from understanding the times to making the most of the time.

Making the Most of the Time

11

Moments Burdened with Glorious Purpose

O Lord, to what have we come? For a small gain there is toil and hurry, and what is in the highest degree needful is passed negligently by.

Thomas á Kempis, *The Imitation of Christ*

There's diem to carpe!

Cloudy with a Chance of Meatballs

Everything comes to him who hustles while he waits.

Thomas Edison

O swiftly see! Each moment flies!
See and learn, be thinking wise.
Seize the moments as they fly;
Learn to live and know to die.

inscription on an
1840 Shaker wall clock

Your days are numbered. Use them to throw open the windows of your soul to the sun. If you do not, the sun will soon set, and you with it.

Marcus Aurelius, *The Emperor's Handbook*

As if you could kill time without injuring eternity.

Henry David Thoreau, *Walden*

Our family loves to watch the Indianapolis Colts. We especially enjoyed watching during Peyton Manning's reign as quarterback. He was masterful in a number of areas, but one particular strength was his leadership during the two-minute drill.

Obviously, every one of the sixty minutes of a game requires effective play, and every play counts. When you have the ball, you have to run, block, pass, and catch well, and when the other team has the ball, you need to thwart their attack with a strong defensive line, close coverage of receivers, and effective tackles.

But during the last two minutes of a closely contested game, especially when the team with the ball is losing, everything changes. Playing a hurry-up offense, the team runs through a sequence of plays that have been carefully practiced beforehand. Every player knows just what he is supposed to do next. There are no huddles; the players go right back to the line after each play. If the quarterback doesn't like the way the defense lines up against him, he adjusts the play on the spot, turning to his players and calling out the change.

By skipping huddles, the team conserves time and wears out the defense. They also increase their chance of keeping possession of the ball and limit loss of time by throwing safe passes toward the sidelines, where receivers can catch the ball and then step out of bounds, stopping the clock. During the last two minutes of the game, the goal is clear and shapes everything: get into the end zone and win the game.

The parallels with the Christian life are intriguing.

Here's the Drill

In an earlier chapter, we explored the fact that our time on earth is short. The biblical writers use the expressions "the day is coming" and "the hour is coming" to underscore life's brevity. In this chapter, I want to unfold the phrase "while there is time." This expression, filled with urgency, presses us to consider the implications of that brevity. What things should we be about in the time we have left? This is how Paul expressed it to the church in Ephesus: "Be very careful, then, how you live—not as unwise but as wise, making the most of every *kairos*" (Eph. 5:15–16).

If we rightly understand the times, we realize the clock is running down. It's time for the two-minute drill. But what are our assignments during this hurry-up offense? How do we make the most of the time?

Scripture identifies four things that God wants us to have on our hearts in this swift-passing life, concerns that should shape how we live while there is time.

Come to Faith

First, we are urged *now* to get right with God. Our relationship with God towers in importance over every other dimension of life. Marriage, family, career, health, finances all take a distant second. Scripture commands us to reflect on our sin and rebellion against God, to turn from a life lived for self, and to entrust our lives to Christ by faith while there is time.

> Let all the godly pray to you while there is still time,
> that they may not drown in the floodwaters of judgment. (Ps. 32:6 NLT)

Trust in the light while there is still time. (John 12:36 NLT)

Can't you see how kind God has been in giving you time to turn from your sin? (Rom. 2:4 NLT (1996 version); see also 2 Pet. 3:9, 15)

> We implore you on Christ's behalf: Be reconciled to God. . . . I tell
> you, now is the time of God's favor, now is the day of salvation.
> (2 Cor. 5:20; 6:2)

Soon we will die, or Christ will return. When the window closes, whether on our life or on the present age, it will no longer be possible to be reconciled to God. And if we have not placed the full weight of our confidence on Jesus by that moment, we will be closed out from the Lord's presence in the age to come and will spend eternity apart from him—a gulf of hellish magnitude.

In his *Confessions*, Augustine describes how he repeatedly deferred the decision to follow Christ: "'Just a minute,' 'One more minute,' 'Let me have a little longer.' But these 'minutes' never diminished, and my 'little longer' lasted indefinitely long."[1] After long postponing his response to grace and feeling his soul "torn apart" by the tug of truth at his will, Augustine finally relented: "'Let it be now,' I was saying to myself. 'Now is the moment, let it be now.'"[2]

Believe in Jesus now, while there is time.

Grow in Faith

If choosing to enter into a relationship with God through faith in Christ is the single most important decision of our lives, then the way we tend that relationship and the way we conduct ourselves in it will be our greatest daily concern. Paul sums up that conduct this way: "Be very careful, then, how you live—not as unwise but as wise" (Eph. 5:15).

"Making good choices" is how we talked about wisdom with our kids when they were young. But in Scripture, "wisdom" has a narrower meaning. It is shorthand for a way of living that honors God and includes him, while "folly" is a way of life that ignores God and thumbs its nose at him.

Wise living assumes an ongoing commitment to our growth in godliness. Deepening our relationship with God becomes our first concern as we seek to integrate our faith into all aspects of our lives, maturing "in speech, in conduct, in love, in faith and in purity" (1 Tim. 4:12) and allowing Christ more and more to live his life through us (Gal. 2:20). Paul captures this emphasis on a life that pleases God in his first letter to the church in Corinth:

> The time that remains is very short. . . . Spend [your] time doing the Lord's work and thinking how to please him. . . . I want you to do whatever will help you serve the Lord best, with as few distractions as possible. (7:29, 32, 35 NLT)

Each day, and each part of each day, presents us with a choice. We can "be diligent in these matters; [giving ourselves] wholly to them, so that everyone may see [our] progress" (1 Tim. 4:15). Or we can waste our time, foolishly frittering away our God-given time on any number of misguided pursuits that displace God from his rightful place in our lives: "Do not waste time arguing over godless ideas and old wives' tales. Instead, train yourself to be godly. Physical training is good, but training for godliness is much better, promising benefits in this life and in the life to come" (1 Tim. 4:7–8 NLT).

God does not merely give us time. He gives us time *for*. Time comes to us as a trust and carries with it a stewardly responsibility. Time can be spent well, or it can be wasted, which is to say, from God's vantage point, it can be spent rightly or wrongly. While there is still time, we need to spend our time cultivating a relationship with the Lord and growing in godliness.

Live Our Faith

In addition to calling us to seek God now and serve him always, God places opportunities for ministry and mission before us at *certain* times.

139

Opportunities are not in our control. We don't bring them about. They come to us from outside. But how we respond to opportunities *is* in our control. Wrapped up in time's embrace come opportunities that can be capitalized on or squandered. This language comes forcefully into Jesus's speech when, with tears, he says to the people of Jerusalem, "You have missed the opportunity God offered you" (Luke 19:44, author's trans.).

We are called to make the most of such opportunities, which are of two sorts: living our faith and sharing our faith.

First, as God gives us opportunity, we are called to do good.

Whenever we have the opportunity, we should do good. (Gal. 6:10 NLT)

Be ready to do whatever is good. (Titus 3:1)

Make the most of every opportunity in these evil days. (Eph. 5:16 NLT)

"Doing good" is the essential ethic of the kingdom (1 Pet. 2:21) and the essential mark of its subjects (3 John 11). As Paul urged his protégé Titus, "Our people must learn to devote themselves to doing what is good" (Titus 3:14).

The history of the Christian church's engagement with the surrounding culture, while including some lamentable chapters, is largely the history of the church's faithfulness to this call—seeking the good of the city in which God has placed it (Jer. 29:7). At different places in different eras, loving neighbors and doing good has meant fighting poverty and crime, starting hospitals and schools, caring for widows and orphans, redressing abuse, correcting neglect, and promoting reform.

Day by day God places us in circumstances meant to bring forth the good for which we were made and called: "We are God's handiwork, created in Christ Jesus to do good works, which God prepared in advance for us to do" (Eph. 2:10). Doing good is part of God's divine design for us.

Luke 6, one of many chapters in Scripture devoted to the theme of doing good, describes us as cups so full of grace that we cannot help but spill over into the lives of others. Jesus hints that when we show love, speak encouragement, serve others, meet needs, love enemies—the grace we have received from God sloshing over the rim of our lives into the dry cups of others—we make most obvious our family resemblance to our heavenly Father as his children (Luke 6:27–38). Whenever we live out our faith in tangible acts of good, we mirror God's character, causing God to grow in the estimation of others. As Jesus said to his disciples, "Let your light shine before others, that they may see your good deeds and glorify your Father in heaven" (Matt. 5:16).

Share Our Faith

Second, as God gives us opportunity, we are called to share our faith: to urge others through our words and our lives to give their lives in faith to Christ.

If the most important thing that can happen before we die (or Christ returns) is for us to believe in Jesus, then that is also the most important thing that can happen in the lives of those God has placed around us. And God desires to use us to help bring that about, so he gives us opportunity.

When I came to the city of Troas to preach the Good News of Christ, the Lord opened a door of opportunity for me. (2 Cor. 2:12 NLT)

Live wisely among those who are not believers, and make the most of every opportunity. Let your conversation be gracious and attractive so that you will have the right response for everyone. (Col. 4:5 NLT)

You must warn each other every day, while it is still "today," so that none of you will be deceived by sin and hardened against God. (Heb. 3:13 NLT)

God calls us to look for, expect, and even pray for these God-given opportunities. Colossians 4:3 says, "Pray for us, too, that God will give us many opportunities to speak about his mysterious plan concerning Christ" (NLT).

At times in my life, I prayed that God would give me an opportunity every day to lead someone one step closer to Christ. I've prayed the same for my congregation. When I pray that request, not only do I have great conversations and see others come to Christ, but my own faith also grows in confidence and vibrancy. As Paul wrote to Philemon, "As you share the faith you have in common with others, I pray that you may come to have a complete knowledge of every blessing we have in Christ" (Philem. 6 GW). God, make it so!

How do we make the most of the time we have? We come to faith now, deepen our faith daily, and live our faith and share our faith as God gives us opportunity.

The Play-Calling God

In David Stern's translation of Luke 10:4, as Jesus sends out his disciples to do ministry, he says to them, "Don't stop to *schmoose* with people on the road." Stern explains:

The Yiddish word *schmoose*, which means "talk in a friendly way, chit-chat, engage in idle conversation, gossip," and is derived from Hebrew *shmu'ot* ("things heard, rumors"), conveys precisely the sense of Yeshua's instruction not to waste time on the road but to hasten to the destination and get on with the work to be done.[3]

Urgency and clarity are signs that we understand the *kairos* and seek to make the most of it. But often I substitute busyness and distraction for urgency. And I can wander from thing to thing rather than carrying out my ministry with clarity of purpose.

Think back to the football analogy. Typically all the plays for the two-minute drill are planned, practiced, and committed to memory well ahead of time. We don't need to go to the huddle to find out from the quarterback what plays we should be running; we already know. We've gone over them a hundred times.

By analogy, in these closing minutes of the age, as we take our place at the line of scrimmage, we don't have to turn to the Lord and ask, "What am I supposed to do?" We already have our basic game plan: love and pursue God, love and pursue others. That's 85 percent of the Christian life right there.

But here is where it gets interesting. During the final two minutes of a football game, the quarterback will sometimes turn, look a player in the eye, and signal or audible a specific play he wants him to run that's not part of the two-minute drill. It might be to block a certain defensive player or to run a particular pattern. It might be to receive a handoff or to catch a pass. The player must keep his eyes and ears fixed on the quarterback so that, in the intensity of the game and the hubbub of the stadium, he can hear the call and faithfully run the play.

Notice the similarity to the way God makes his purposes known to his people. While we have the basic game plan, sometimes God delights to direct us in the moment as he sees fit. This is a thrilling and unexpected dimension to making the most of the *kairos*. God doesn't merely hand us a plan. He takes us by the hand and leads us.

On his second missionary journey, trekking across what we know today as Turkey, Paul was redirected twice. First, as he traveled across Galatia and Phrygia, following the primary Roman roads from east to west, he suddenly veered north, "having been kept by the Holy Spirit from preaching the word in the province of Asia" (Acts 16:6).

Then, having traversed the province of Mysia and come to its farthest border, Paul assumed he and his companions would circle back east toward the more familiar world of Anatolia. "But the Spirit of Jesus would not allow them to" (Acts 16:7). Instead, following the leading of the Spirit given to them in a vision, they turned their backs on all that was familiar and headed toward Europe.

God called an audible.

━

Scripture teaches us that during this window of time in which we live, this ever-closing season between the first and second comings of Christ, the Holy Spirit is vibrantly at work among God's people.

He convicts us of sin (John 16:8).

He teaches us the truth (John 16:13).

He calls us to faith (1 Pet. 1:12).

He opens us to God's love (Rom. 5:5).

He brings us to life spiritually (Rom. 8:11).

He indwells us (Rom. 8:9).

And, of particular importance to our discussion here, he *leads* us: "Since we live by the Spirit, let us keep in step with the Spirit" (Gal. 5:25).

During my later childhood years, my father started a Boy Scout troop so he could have consistent time with my brother and me. Once a month, Troop 447 headed out on a hiking and camping trip, often hiking twenty miles or more in a single day. Sometimes I walked immediately behind my dad, timing my pace to his, placing my feet where his had been. When the day grew hot, my feet sore, and my legs weary, my father encouraged me to imagine a rope tied around his waist and mine—and that he was pulling me along.

Keeping in step with the Spirit means we are letting him lead us. He decides the course, sets the pace, leads the way. We put our feet in his footsteps and receive encouragement from his strong and loving presence.

As we've already noted, God breaks into our lives in *kairos* moments—moments freighted with unusual significance that rise to the surface in the current of time each day. These are the very junctures at which we experience God's personal leading. God by his Spirit turns to *me*, calls *my* name, and places an opportunity before *me*. I can experience these nudges and promptings in myriad ways:

when in my quiet time, Bible open, and I hear the voice of conviction

when I sit with my colleague over lunch, and we discuss his uncertain future

when I take out the trash, and my neighbor strolls over for a conversation

when I walk past a homeless man shaking a paper cup with a few coins rattling at the bottom

when I am reminded of a hard or uncomfortable task I have put off

when I hear the tap on the bedroom door, and my son walks in past his curfew

when I ask my daughter about her day, and tears suddenly moisten her eyes

when in a conversation with my wife I am confronted with a pattern of insensitivity or untrustworthiness in my life

when I am moved to indignation when I hear of injustices being done to children in my community when an absent friend is suddenly brought to mind

when worship moves me to tears

when I hear the pain in a friend's voice in the first few moments of a call

when I think—for the fortieth time in the past hour—of a painful circumstance in which I find myself

when a light, everyday conversation at work suddenly shifts to a place of greater depth and vulnerability

In these *kairos* moments, we ask, "God, what opportunity are you putting before me to which you want me to be faithful?"

Holy Potential

Whenever our family goes out to eat, we try to learn our waiter's name and enter into conversation for a bit, just to leave the door open to what God might wish to do. At one restaurant our waitress was a buoyant young woman I'll call Lauren. From time to time during our meal, she stopped by and checked in on us or interacted with the kids, and we had some fun, brief exchanges with her.

When it came time to pay our bill, we told Lauren we thought she had done a great job and said, "God's grace to you"—something that hinted in the smallest way at our faith. When she came back with our credit card, she stopped, her face suddenly got serious, and she said, "Can I ask you something? What is the secret of a happy family?"

How could we sum up the place of God in our lives in a sentence or two? Sharon spoke the just-right words: "We view each of our children as a gift from God and try to treat them in a way that reflects that."

Lauren shot up two thumbs, bobbed her head, and said, "Cool!" Lingering at our table, she told us she'd had a pretty painful childhood. She said she'd seen something different in our family, wondered what it was, and felt compelled to ask.

In subsequent visits, we made a point to request Lauren and got to know her better. Two months later, she moved into our house. One time, sitting in our kitchen, Lauren expressed her fears about becoming a Christian, that it would require her to become a nonperson. Then she said, "But if Christianity is what makes you guys the way you are, that's what I want." Chaos became *kairos*.

Another example. A few years back, our sons and a cousin had a golf cart accident that badly hurt one son's lower leg. We held him while we waited for the ambulance and helped him as much as we could when the EMTs arrived. Then Sharon rode with him in the ambulance. In the hallway of the hospital, we interacted a bit with the EMTs as Brandon was being cared for. Their care for Brandon had been wonderful, and we made a point to communicate that, but our focus, as you would expect, was on Brandon.

A month after the accident, we got a letter from the lead emergency tech. He said that the brief time he spent with us made a real impact on him. After six years of working as an EMT, he finally saw a picture of how a healthy family is meant to work. He thanked us for the way we not only showed love to our son but also took the time to express care and thoughtfulness to him and his team—even as we were in the midst of this crisis.

How humbling! Writing back, we again expressed our gratitude and said that, while it was an accident that had brought us together, we didn't believe it was an accident that we had met. God planned that time because he had a gift for us through him, our EMT, and a gift for him through us. It was God's presence that he had seen in us.

Moments stuffed full of divine import, brimming with holy potential, require of us that they be recognized and that we respond in faithfulness.

Loki, the smarmy villain in the lighthearted movie *The Avengers*, swells with pride and proclaims, "I am Loki of Asgard! And I am burdened with glorious purpose!" While the claim was a bit inflated for Loki, it is not too grand for these set-apart moments. Each comes brimming with holy purpose.

As we go through the day, God is knocking at our door, he is stepping under our roof, he is riding in our car, he is standing by us in line, he is sitting by us in the pew, he is living in the house next door, he is calling us on the phone. He is working in the unfolding course of human events to reveal himself, to bless his people, to advance his kingdom, and to accomplish his loving purposes.

God grant us eyes to see in the cup of a moment the hollow of God's hand.

12

The One Thing

I wish I'd spent more time in the office.

last words of Henry Royce,
cofounder of Rolls-Royce

The aim of life has been forgotten, the end has been left behind. Man has set out at a tremendous speed to go nowhere.

Jacques Ellul, *The Presence of the Kingdom*

Our greatest danger is letting the urgent things crowd out the important ones.

Charles E. Hummel, *Freedom from Tyranny of the Urgent*

If you're too busy to pray, you're too busy.

Anonymous

The greatest competitor of devotion to Jesus is service for Him. "Be careful about one thing only," says our Lord—"your relationship to Me." Beware of any work for God which enables you to evade concentration on Him.

Oswald Chambers, *My Utmost for His Highest*

Colorado Springs, where we lived for nine years, is known for its deep blue skies. But every so often, especially in the winter, we would experience a thermal inversion. A thick, warm layer of brown smog would spread out on top of the city, held in place by a blanket of clear, colder air on top of it. Normally hot air rises, and the smog thrown up by the power plant is carried away by the hot smoke. But in a thermal inversion, everything is upside down. The hot, dirty air sits there, blocking the light of the sun and turning everything a smudgy brown.

Every once in a while, you and I, as followers of Christ, can experience what we might call *priority inversion*. The most important things get reversed with a host of lesser things, creating a cloud of distraction, and we lose sight of God.

One early morning, I was running out the door for work, already feeling crunched, when my sweet wife grabbed my arm and pulled me to a stop.

"How about if we pray?" she said.

"Let's make it fast," I answered. "On the inside of me I hear a great big tick-tick-tick."

"Lord," she prayed, "thank you that you are the Lord of the tick-tick-tick, of the clutter within our souls. We stop to acknowledge you, to remember that you are Lord of our days and that everything we do we do for you. Lead us, Lord, in the things you would have us do to serve and honor you today."

Oh yeah, I thought as I climbed in my car, *this is all about him. Kinda makes sense to include him in it.*

Unconventional Wisdom

One day, Jesus drops in on the home of two sisters, Martha and Mary. Martha, the older sister, invites Jesus in, opening up a fascinating encounter recorded for us in Luke 10. In this brief exchange, Jesus overthrows conventions and assumptions with as much vigor and resolve as when he flipped over the merchants' tables in the temple. As we wrestle with how to find balance in a busy world, this story is crucial.

Martha scurries about, preparing a feast for Jesus and doing everything she can to express how glad she is to have him under her roof. But her younger sister, Mary, neglects her responsibilities, which incites Martha to indignation and moves her to bring her frustration to Jesus.

> She had a sister called Mary, who sat at the Lord's feet listening to what he said. But Martha was distracted by all the preparations that had to be made. She came to him and asked, "Lord, don't you care that my sister has left me to do the work by myself? Tell her to help me!"
>
> "Martha, Martha," the Lord answered, "you are worried and upset about many things, but few things are needed—or indeed only one. Mary has chosen what is better, and it will not be taken from her." (Luke 10:39–42)

We look back on this story from our twenty-first-century vantage point and wonder how Martha could have been so blind, slavishly puttering about in the kitchen while the King of kings sat in her family room.

But that's not how a person from Jesus's place and time would react to this story. In order to hear how jolting and unexpected Jesus's words would have been to Martha, Mary, and the disciples, we need to know more about three things: the place of hospitality in the Middle East, the treatment a rabbi typically received as a guest in someone's home, and the traditional view of women in Jesus's day.

Hospitality toward a stranger is one of the highest social values in the Middle East, and it always has been. Opening your home to a stranger is perhaps the greatest of all virtues. In Jesus's time, it was also an obligation. In a harsh desert land, you never knew when you might find yourself lost and destitute, in need of food and shelter for which you could not pay. You freely gave to others what you knew you might one day need yourself.

If the value of hospitality was high throughout the Middle East, this was especially true of the Jewish people. For them, it was not only social custom or potential need that drove them to hospitality. It was also the command of the Torah. Leviticus 19 says, "The foreigner residing among you must be treated as your native-born. Love them as yourself, for you were foreigners in Egypt" (v. 34).

The stakes rose when the person on your doorstep was a religious leader. Rabbis who were Jesus's contemporaries had very specific opinions about hospitality. Some Jewish teachers believed it was even more important than studying the Torah.[1] And they were not shy about pointing out that they believed it was especially praiseworthy to practice hospitality toward a rabbi.[2] Nor were they reluctant to spell out just how to entertain. The proper host will look pleased while entertaining his guests, he will wait upon them himself, he will promise little and give much, and so on. Meanwhile, the proper guest will make a point to acknowledge everything that the person has done for him, saying, "At what trouble my host has been, and all for my sake!" and he will not refuse anything that is offered to him.[3]

It's also helpful to note one other convention of the day. While men were seen as deserving special honor, women were viewed as worthy of no honor at all; they were mere workers, on par with servants. We see this division in children's schooling. Many boys and girls attended *beth sefer*, the first stage of school, until the age of twelve. After that age, the girls returned home to learn homemaking skills and to get ready for marriage, while many of the boys stayed on for the next level of school, called *beth midrash*. Then, at age fifteen, most of the boys finished school and started to learn a trade. But a few of the very brightest boys—no girls—would continue on to the final stage of school, called *beth talmud.* In this stage of their education, they would join up with a particular rabbi and follow him as his disciple.

With his response to Mary and Martha, Jesus upends society's idea of what it means to be a good hostess, a good woman, a good guest, and a good rabbi, and he redefines what it means to be a good disciple.

To Martha he says that spending three hours in the kitchen whipping up a five-star meal for the thirteen of them is not the best way to honor and serve him. While he is grateful for her effort, he would rather have her spend the time *with* him than bustle about on his behalf.

He says to the disciples that, contrary to what they have heard from other rabbis, he does not wish anyone to go to great lengths for him. He is not there to be served but to serve.

And to Mary, who has abandoned the kitchen and taken a place with the twelve disciples, he says that she is not being the least bit presumptuous by placing herself as an equal to men at his feet. She is just where he wants her to be.

The message is clear. God is more concerned about the time we spend with him than the things we do for him. As Evelyn Underhill writes, "Man's first duty is adoration; and his second duty is awe; and only his third duty is service."[4]

The Relational Life

Jesus doesn't want us to make a fuss for him. He just wants us to spend time with him, sitting at his feet. For the past three months or so, I've been using Psalm 143:8–11 to begin my time with the Lord. Before I open anything, I open my heart to the Lord by prayerfully walking through the passage from memory:

> Let me hear of your unfailing love each morning,
>> for I am trusting you.

Show me where to walk,
  for I give myself to you.
Rescue me from my enemies, LORD;
  I run to you to hide me.
Teach me to do your will,
  for you are my God.
May your gracious Spirit lead me forward
  on a firm footing.
For the glory of your name, O LORD. (NLT)

Cultivating a love relationship with God matters to him more than anything else. This is the first and greatest commandment, the thing we must do before we do anything else: simply to love the Lord our God with the whole of our being (Matt. 22:37–38).

Sometimes we equate love with service, thinking we must show Jesus our love through our actions. But Jesus wants us to place our relationship with him *ahead* of our service for him.

It's interesting that Luke 10:40 says, "Martha was distracted by all the preparations that *had* to be made." But who said they had to be made? Not Jesus. Martha is caught up in doing good works that *she* has prepared in advance to do, not that God prepared for her to do.

Charles Spurgeon said, "Her fault was not that she served. The condition of a servant well becomes every Christian. Her fault was that she grew 'cumbered with much serving,' so that she forgot him and only remembered the service."[5]

As modern Westerners who secretly take pride in the busyness we so constantly complain about, this is a huge temptation for us. Joanna Weaver writes, "We get caught up in the performance trap, feeling as though we must prove our love for God by doing great things for him. So we rush past the intimacy of the Living Room to get busy for him in the Kitchen."[6]

There's a story about a bunch of pastors who are spending the day at a prayer retreat. In the middle of the morning, during a break, some of the pastors are sitting by the window, enjoying creation and having a leisurely conversation. Then one of them notices Jesus walking up the road toward them. He turns to the person next to him, grabs his arm, and whispers, "Jesus is coming! What should we do?" The other man's face whitens; he hops up from his seat and blurts out, "Quick, look busy!"

If we conceive of ourselves as important to God only when we are getting something done for him, our walk of faith will become a weary walk of works. That's just the sort of priority inversion from which Jesus means to rescue us.

First and Last

Our staff has heard me say often that we have no business coming in to serve God if we haven't first spent time with him, inviting him to order our hearts and our days. But too often that is the very thing I do.

I remember one season several years ago. Feeling the crunch of things to be done with a short staff and, if I'm honest, feeling the need to prove my competence and effectiveness, I let my work nibble into time reserved for prayer, study, spiritual retreats, and other practices that feed my soul and draw me to God. I started going to work a bit sooner and staying a bit later, and I plunked my disciplines on the shelf for a bit.

A bit. How we minimize the truth we tell ourselves.

For months, I tuned out that mysterious glug-glug-glug sound. Then I found myself sitting low and sluggish in the water, with a soul malnourished and paper-thin, with a body sick and run-down, and with a mind cluttered and struggling to focus on a single point. I had quite efficiently scuttled myself.

Serving Jesus can get in the way of our relationship with him. In his classic devotional guide, Oswald Chambers challenges us on just this point: "The great enemy to the Lord Jesus Christ in the present day is the conception of practical work . . . in which endless energy and activities are insisted upon, but no private life with God."[7] Ouch. Jesus tells us the same thing. "There is only one thing worth being concerned about" (Luke 10:42 NLT).

Sometimes creation has a way of making plain a spiritual principle that we manage to complicate. One day as I prayed outdoors, I noticed how intent was every tree and leaf upon the light that broke through the canopy overhead. The more I looked, the more I realized that every aspect of the tree's shape and foliage traced back to this one hunger for one thing. Wondering that my life did not reflect that same single pursuit, I wrote this:

Heliotrope

One gap only
in the shadowed canopy
And to that one gap, that one appalling lapse,
does every gasping leaf turn.

What deserves the best of our attention? What matters more than anything else? Him. Not our scrambling efforts on his behalf but his glorious reign over us, and over all.

13

Waiting

Instant gratification takes too long.

Twitter post by Carrie Fisher

It's good to hope. It's the waiting that spoils it.

Yiddish proverb

I prayed, but the prayers were tangled and dissenting. I prayed the Lord would sort them out and answer as needed. Above all that He would hurry.

Leif Enger, *Peace like a River*

The trouble is that I'm in a hurry, but God isn't.

Phillips Brooks

Waiting patiently in expectation is the foundation of the spiritual life.

Simone Weil, *First and Last Notebooks*

These things I plan won't happen right away. Slowly, steadily, surely, the time approaches when the vision will be fulfilled. If it seems slow, wait patiently, for it will surely take place. It will not be delayed.

Habakkuk 2:3 TLB

My ear, stopped up with fluid, rings and pulses with every heartbeat. Pressure builds, then—as I hold my breath and swallow and wriggle my jaw—it eases, only to build again. The sound of ringing phones and clattering dishes bounces torturously through my ear's chamber, maxing out my hearing like the speaker on a cheap AM radio. My thinking is fuzzy, my patience is thin, people feel oddly removed, and I just want to be alone.

Ten days of this is driving me nuts.

Part of my exasperation is that these ten days coincide with my kids' school vacations. I'm coming off a full fall, when ministry demands often pulled me away from my family. Now I finally have time to build snowmen and watch home videos and play Ping-Pong with my kids or to sit in front of the fire or go to a movie with my wife, and I feel miserable. On top of that, I finally have time to work on my book, and it's the last thing I feel like doing. I'm challenged pulling together a shopping list let alone a string of coherent sentences.

The solution to a life of busyness, we've said, is to do those relatively few things to which God calls us, when and how he directs us, and to trust him with the rest. But what happens when we can't do *anything*? When, for whatever reason, we can't move forward and the passing of time haunts us with a sense of uselessness, of purposelessness? Then what?

Hating Waiting

Motion is the great American virtue, and waiting is the ultimate un-American act.

Look at us in checkout lines. Well, look at *me* in checkout lines. From the moment I round the end of an aisle, my last product in hand, I begin calculating which is the speediest lane. I study the number of items in each person's cart. I scrutinize the clerks and shoppers in each row, gauging how fast-moving or inefficient, how chatty or taciturn, each is likely to be. I select my line accordingly. Then I monitor the other lines to make sure I'm in the fastest one, even hopping from line to line if I think I can get out more quickly.

You may have heard of Skinner's Law: "The other line always moves faster." Perhaps you've also heard of Jenkins's Corollary: "However, when you switch to another line, the line you left moves faster." To these could be added the Henderson Counter-Corollary: "Whichever line you are in, the more you think about how slow it is, the slower it gets."

Mind Your Peace and Queues

Our impatient human nature has given rise to a school of thought known as queue management, which is all about easing the strain on customers waiting in line. Mathematicians have studied various line configurations (mob, take a number, single line, multiple lines) and have calculated the best way to improve speed, shorten waits, and ensure first-come-first-served and first-in-first-out service.

Meanwhile, psychologists have explored the feelings and responses related to waiting that lead to such behavior as airline passengers remaining seated contentedly for the duration of a three-hour flight but scrambling to get into the aisles the moment the plane comes to a stop. To forestall impatience, waiting-line consultants suggest giving exaggerated wait estimates to restaurant customers; providing mirrors, magazines, menus, and televisions to occupy those waiting; using frequent communication to ease anxiety and uncertainty; and clustering those who are waiting into groups to create "community" among the similarly inconvenienced.

We experienced one such method on the Splash Mountain log flume at Disney World in Orlando. It had become our favorite ride, and we were on our third time through when we suddenly found ourselves jolted to a stop in the dark chute just before the final plunge.

There we sat, the six of us—five minutes, ten minutes, fifteen minutes—waiting while they fixed the ride, our wait punctuated every three minutes by Br'er Bear saying, "Looks like Br'er Fox and Br'er Rabbit are causin' some kinda commotion downstream. You just sit tight till we figger out what the problem is." Guess how much we enjoyed that. All these years later, the line still comes up in conversation with our kids, so ingrained is it in all of our heads.

When I am made to wait, I feel I am being diminished, that something is being taken from me. Traffic jam, post office line, doctor's office waiting room—it's all the same. I feel as though I begin leaking away when I am made to wait. Did you notice that word *made*? Waiting is less about stopping than being made to stop. There's the rub.

Effective Inefficiency

When most of us think of waiting, we think of *wasting* time. Waiting can only be endured, not redeemed. But the Bible's view of waiting is markedly different.

"As the heavens are higher than the earth, so are my ways higher than your ways," declares the Lord (Isa. 55:9). A couple of days ago in my quiet time, I reread those words, noticing their context for the first time. They come at the start of that image-rich section in which God describes how he bears fruit in our lives. His Word will come down from heaven and will not return to him empty but will accomplish what he desires, achieving the purpose for which it was sent (Isa. 55:10–13).

Rain comes down from the heavens and *slowly* seeps down to the seed that lies buried, out of sight. The kernel *slowly* pushes out a root to drink the life-giving moisture. *Slowly* the budding plant sends up a shoot to break the soil and drink the light. The shoot *slowly* grows into a stalk, and *slowly* the stalk sprouts grain, and the grain *slowly* ripens. What takes a single verse to describe takes half a year to bring about.

When we're hungry, we want food now! But sometimes God means to keep us hungry longer so that he might truly *satisfy* us and not merely feed us. He doesn't just want to give us something; he wants to grow us *into* something. God is determined to remake and transform us from glory to glory into the likeness of Christ (2 Cor. 3:18). One of his most effective transformative tools is a season of waiting.

When we are made to wait, it does not mean God is overlooking something. It means God is *overseeing* something. Waiting is not a place where God fails us; it is where he meets us.

During a season of waiting in my life, I came across a biblical pattern that has stretched and encouraged me ever since: God seems to delight in imposing a time of waiting on those he intends to use.

- Joseph, still carrying the promise of his dream, sat in a dark sandstone cell for ten years.
- Moses, raised and trained among royalty, wandered the desert chasing a flock of sheep for forty years.
- David, after being crowned king but before taking his throne, ran back and forth across the wilderness hiding from raving Saul for seven years.
- Paul, newly converted and already informed of his world-changing mission, was led into the Desert of Arabah for three years.

Not just once but regularly God seemed to do this. What was he thinking? What a waste! Kingdom concerns are too pressing to bench your players for years at a time.

When I came out of seminary at twenty-eight, I applied to a number of churches, all of them between five hundred and a thousand members, most of them looking for a senior pastor. I convinced myself I was prepared to serve in such a role. Others had repeatedly affirmed my leadership and communication gifts, plus I'd had the benefit of a unique, yearlong, pre-seminary internship in a large church.

My search came down to two positions: the senior pastor of a good-sized church and the associate pastor of a small new church. I, of course, knew which God had for me. But I was wrong. As Sharon and I drove up the hill to say good-bye to the pastor of the smaller church, ready to head for the senior role, we both sensed that God was saying, "David, right now I'm more concerned with what I am going to do *in* you than what I am going to do *through* you, and this is where I want to do it."

For the next nine years, God went to work on my pride, drawing into the light my overly large view of myself and gently whittling me back to life-size. He used Tom to tell me my preaching was boring, Steve to tell me I was missing my audience, John to tell me my messages weren't sufficiently Christ-centered, Doug to tell me I was cocky and always seemed to have to be right, and Terry to tell me I was unapproachable. Meanwhile, God used frustrations in my relationship with the senior pastor to teach me patience, humility, flexibility, and understanding.

Coming out of seminary, I *needed* to be a senior pastor: I needed to be known, to be respected and admired, to make a difference, to be in charge, to use my gifts. What drove my need, of course, was my reliance on my role and the opinion of others to provide the significance that could come only from God.

After nine rather uncomfortable years with Christ in the school of humility, I had largely laid aside my ambition. I didn't *need* to serve as a senior pastor anymore. My heart was content, my soul at rest.

That's what God was waiting for. Once I didn't *need* it, God knew I was truly ready to do it. He called me to serve as the senior pastor of a sizeable church, and I was free to say yes, not to meet some need of mine but simply to answer God's call.

What is the soil in which the fruit of the Spirit is grown if not waiting? Love, joy, peace, patience, kindness, goodness, gentleness, faithfulness, self-control—every one is the fruit of waiting. In waiting, I learn to love those I don't like, to find joy in God rather than in circumstances, to be at peace with matters outside my control, to be patient with annoyances, to be kind to the weak and struggling, to pursue goodness rather than ambition, to let God grow large as I recede into a spirit of gentle humility, to be faithful to what is before me regardless of how little I enjoy it or benefit from it, and to let God, rather than my feelings, control me.

In this light, from God's vantage point, those periods of benching his players begin to make sense. Moses's temper and proneness to take things into his own hands, Joseph's brashness and insensitivity to the feelings of others, Paul's recklessness and readiness to fight, and David's independence and concern for self needed to be scoured away in a season of prolonged waiting.

It isn't just *what* we do. It's *how* we do it. It's *who we are* as we do it. I little understood that fresh out of seminary. Now I'm convinced that what God desires to do *in* us is every bit as important as anything he might do *through* us.

Sharon recently gave me the gift of a deep tissue massage at a local spa. Now, a relaxation massage is delightful, but deep tissue massage can't really be described that way. It hurts, but it reaches into deeper muscle areas that have become rigid with ill use and stress and slowly works them into restored flexibility. Waiting times are the spiritual equivalent of deep tissue massage, working those stubborn and resistant areas that regular spiritual disciplines just can't reach.

Ultimately, waiting shifts our focus from the things we want God to do to the things God wants to do, and so often the things God is most keen to do lie within us. That's why waiting is not the exception in the Christian life. It is the norm. We are asked by God to wait all the time, for our good.

Weighting

We tend to think of waiting as waiting *until*—until the light changes, until the line moves, until the fever breaks, until the shift ends. Waiting *until* is usually a time of antsy impatience, of drumming fingers and jouncing feet and muttered c'mon, c'mon, c'mons. Waiting is enduring.

This idea is inadvertently reinforced by the way most Bible translations handle the phrase "wait for the Lord." We wait for slow busses and busy waiters and tardy checks—for things that are late. But when Scripture invites us to "wait for the LORD" (Ps. 27:14), it intends more than knotted-up, anxious, clock-watching impatience. It means something much closer to "standing on." That's why I prefer the KJV translation: "Wait on the LORD."

Hebrew poetry (in which the Psalms and much of the Prophets were written) can strike us at times as clunky and labored with its endless restatement. But one of the gifts of poetic parallelism is that it sometimes allows us to understand a message more clearly by stating the same idea again in a different way.

Notice the unexpected synonyms for "waiting on the LORD." Merely enduring isn't one of them.

First, we wait on the Lord when we *seek* him—when we turn to him and pray to him about whatever we're facing, when we ask for his help and invite him in, allowing him to direct us. Psalm 40:1 says, "I waited patiently for the LORD; he turned to me and heard my cry."

When we wait in the biblical sense, we turn our eyes from the face of the clock to the face of our Lord, searching for him, his will, his provision, the fulfillment of his purposes as time passes.

Second, we wait on the Lord when we *yield* to him, relinquishing our lives to him and allowing him to have his way. There is not much point in seeking God if we haven't cleared room in our heart for him to move. As Psalm 37:34 says, "Wait on the LORD and keep his way" (KJV).

Waiting on the Lord means shifting from "I decide" to "you decide," from "I am in charge" to "you are in charge," from "I am king" to "you are King." Waiting on the Lord requires that we *altar* our plans, not alter them. We *altar* them by laying them on the altar, giving them back to God and allowing him to do with them what he wills. Romans 12:1–2 makes plain that only as we offer ourselves back to God as living sacrifices will we be able to "test and approve what God's will is—his good, pleasing and perfect will."

Finally, we wait on the Lord when we *depend* on him, trusting him to do what is best. Isaiah 8:17 says, "I will wait for the LORD. . . . I will put my trust in him."

Waiting does not mean biding our time but abiding in our Lord, in the confidence that he will work things out in his time. We do not *wait until* but *depend upon*, sliding our confidence off of ourselves and placing the weight of our lives onto him, counting on him to step in and act.

As I was studying to speak for a men's retreat a few years ago, I came across a connection that was striking to me. The familiar words of Psalm 46:10, "*Be still*, and know that I am God," are more literally translated "loosen your grip." This is the same verb used in Deuteronomy 31:6 when it says, "The LORD your God goes with you; he will never leave you nor forsake [loosen his grip on] you." God has us in his grip. We can let go of everything else because he is clinging to us.

The notion of waiting evokes for most of us a picture of exasperating passivity. Clinging, however, is a profoundly active posture. When we cling, we actively lay hold of God, actively listen for his voice, actively entrust our burden into his hands, actively shift confidence from ourselves or our circumstances to God. This kind of waiting is anything but passive.

We also typically see waiting in horizontal terms—a delay in our forward progress. We measure waiting in miles and minutes that stand between us and our goal. But waiting from a biblical perspective is vertical—depending upon God in our shortfall. It is measured in terms of posture, not progress—yielding, relinquishing, trusting in him rather than relying on ourselves. From this perspective, waiting is the strong stand of hope, the muscular confidence of faith.

An impish older man in our congregation told me once that he got so fed up with waiting for proper service from a national manufacturing company that he tracked down the CEO's private phone number and called him at three in the morning to complain.

Obviously that isn't the right way to take care of a problem with a broken toaster. But from a spiritual perspective, he got it right. Let your waiting take you straight to the top, to the Lord of heaven and earth. Talk to him about your problems. And then count on him to answer when and how he will.

"Be still before the LORD and wait patiently for him" (Ps. 37:7).

Trusting God with the Rest

14

Soul Rest

I am, you anxious one.

Rainer Rilke,
The Book of Hours

Anxiety is the natural result when our hopes center in anything short of God and his will for us.

Billy Graham, "The Cure for Anxiety"

If you try to seize the day, the day will eventually break you. Seize the corner of his garment and don't let go until he blesses you. He will reshape the day.

Paul Miller, *A Praying Life*

O God Most High, Most Glorious,
    the thought of thine infinite security cheers me,
    for I am toiling and moiling,
    troubled and distressed,
    but thou art forever at perfect peace.

Puritan prayer

You have made us for yourself, O Lord, and our hearts are restless until they find their rest in you.

Augustine, *Confessions*

A few years ago, after a disrupted night of sleep worrying about all the details of life that I was not managing particularly well, I wrote this.

> My soul finds rest
> each day the press the weight
> the burden of the now the next accumulate
> there is always more to do always more
> never enough time there is never enough
>
> My soul finds rest
> yellowing mounds of bank statements
> stacks of magazines half-read the project piles waiting
> to be finished lists of things to do that accumulate
> and accuse fading records of my failure
>
> My soul finds rest
> when does it stop where will it end
> when will I get ahead of it when will it cease
> to be a burden that gnaws away the
> corners of my life my joy my peace
>
> My soul finds rest in God alone

The Rest of the Story

I'm accustomed, when I look out at the bird feeder in our backyard, to seeing fretful, flitful motion without cease—birds darting in, perching on the feeder roof, hopping down to the tray, taking quick jabs at the seed between anxious looks, and then darting off. The smaller the bird, the more frantic the scanning of skies and trees for hawk or cat.

Imagine, then, my utter surprise when, one day last week, I glanced out and saw eight goldfinches perched on the feeder, all utterly still. Each was puffed up into a ball of warmth and complacent ease, head pulled in, body still. Not a neck stretched, not a feather flapped, not a head spun about. Not one clamored for food or scanned the skies. No nervous fidgeting, no frantic darting about. Just . . . rest. In the early chill, they knew no predators were about; they *knew* they were safe.

Security that quiets activity is exactly the picture God gives us of what it means to be at rest in him.

After learning what it means to understand the times and to make the most of the time, we come now to the final part of the tranquility solution: to trust God with the rest.

David wrote in Psalm 23:1–2, "The LORD is my shepherd; I have all that I need. He lets me rest in green meadows; he leads me beside peaceful streams" (NLT). Think of the implications of those words.

First, we *need* rest. In the metaphor of the psalm, we're not the competent shepherd; we're the helpless sheep, anxious for food, fearful of enemies, plagued by everything from wolves to gnats. Our shepherd understands far better than we how wearisome a venture life is and how desperately we need to cease our scrambling.

Second, God means to *give* us rest. He leads us out of anxious striving and into havens of stillness. Rest is a gift from the Creator to his creatures. Let me say that again: rest is a gift from God.

Third, there is ample reason to release our grip and *receive* the gift of rest. Look back at the first verse of the psalm. Because our shepherd is so strong, so capable, so attentive to our needs, we don't have to be. We can rest in the confidence of his care for us. Because all things hold together in *him*—even when it doesn't seem that way—we can let go. He can tend to all the things we can't get to.

There is a busyness that comes of much outward activity. For that, there is a rest grounded in stopping, in ceasing activity, which is the focus of a later chapter.

But there is also an *inner* busyness, a distracted churning of mind that keeps us never still, regardless of how quiet we are outwardly. For that, there is a soul rest that comes not from decreasing activity but from increasing trust. This is the sort of inner rest of which the psalmist speaks when he writes in Psalm 116:7, "Return to your rest, my soul, for the LORD has been good to you."

God wants our waiting to seep over into trusting and our trusting to spill over into resting.

Restive Souls

The relationship between trust and rest is painted in a beautiful set of word pictures near the end of Deuteronomy. God has just summoned Moses to the top of Mount Nebo, where his life will soon come to an end. Before he sets out on his last journey, in the tradition of the Israelites, Moses speaks a blessing over the people, going tribe by tribe. Coming to Benjamin, he imparts these words of peace: "Let the beloved of the LORD rest secure in him, for he shields him all day long, and the one the LORD loves rests between his shoulders" (Deut. 33:12). Three words from this blessing are worth exploring more deeply.

Secure

The Hebrew word for "rest secure" means "to settle in, to dwell." Secure rest comes when we are confident that we have taken up residence in a safe place; we are protected and sheltered, out of harm's reach. "Whoever *dwells* in the shelter of the Most High will *rest* in the shadow of the Almighty" (Ps. 91:1, italics added). We are still because we are safe; we are safe because we are home. When we trust God, we inhabit his trustworthiness.

Secure rest is the opposite of flitting. Flitting is the essence of anxiousness. When I get overwhelmed, my mind hops from one thing on my overflowing to-do list to another, while my heart darts from fear to weariness to overwhelmedness and back to fear. Where do I land my anxious heart? Where do I take up residence and rest?

Abide and *abode* are sister words. We rest in what we dwell in. Want to know where I find peace? Find out where I live. "Lord, through all the generations you have been our home," sings the psalmist (Ps. 90:1 NLT).

In the musical adaptation of Victor Hugo's novel *Les Miserables*, paroled convict Jean Valjean finds shelter for the night under the roof of a gracious bishop. When Valjean tells him, "I have no home," Monseigneur Bienvenu responds, "Then let this be your home." God means for us to make our abode in him. "Let *me* be your home."

Shields

The word *shields* in the next line of the blessing has behind it a strikingly specific image. In the ancient Near East, when making curtains or repairing garments, people would surround weak, worn, or lesser-quality material with fabric that was stronger or of better quality. The frayed and worn were overlaid with the new and sturdy, wrapping up the weakness in their strength. The word *shields* describes that joining of strength to weakness.

The same word is used for the cloth suspended over a bride and groom in a Jewish wedding, representing God's covering, his shielding presence. Not our weakness but his strength, not our shortcomings but his presence determine our well-being and hope.

I remember the painful first few years of ministry at the church where I presently serve. The senior pastor I followed had started the church six months before I was born. For thirty-eight years, the members had known only one approach to ministry—an approach very different from my own. Our "honeymoon" seemed to last about a week, and then the criticism began.

That was when I developed the organ transplant theory of leadership transition: whenever a new pastor comes to a church, part of the body accepts the transplant, and part of the body rejects it. I wasn't sure which side would win out.

At the nadir, amid a steady diet of criticism, I headed off for a few days of retreat to seek clarity about God's calling. Was this the end? I feared it was. Was it time to look elsewhere?

But as soon as I got away and began to listen, I realized that my eyes were fixed in altogether the wrong place. I was focused on the challenging setting I was in instead of on God and his sovereign rule over my life. I was viewing my circumstances as though they, and not God, were determinative.

Thinking back over the past months, I noticed that essentially every time I had received a harsh call or a biting letter about something I had said or done or decided, I had also received a call or a letter, usually on the same day, from someone expressing support over the exact same thing. When I finally saw it, I laughed. Here I was fearful, anxious to please, thinking that others' opinions of me would somehow determine my fate, when God delighted to show me that I was wasting my time trying to please everyone. I didn't need to be anxious that either my shortcomings and the church's impatience or my successes and the church's approval would write the future. I just needed to be faithful to him and to his call on my life. He would take care of the rest.

Seeing afresh that God's strength was sufficient for my inadequacy, I resigned from scrambling and returned from that retreat with freedom and peace. Trust bred rest.

Shoulders

What does it mean, in the final line of the blessing, to rest between God's shoulders? We rest between someone's shoulders when we are folded into their arms and held in their embrace.

It's a picture of strength and intimacy combined, which together bring rest and peace.

Our kids were going through their memory boxes over Christmas break, and my youngest, Corrie, now a beautiful young woman, pulled out a Polaroid picture that had been taken a dozen years before.

"Dad! Remember this?" she said. Sharon and I had led a week-long family camp at Glen Eyrie, and the girls, just three or four years old, were sometimes separated from us when they participated in activities of their own, causing them some anxiousness. So I had had a picture taken of me holding each of my girls and hugging them. Then I had given it to them. "Sometimes we have to be apart," I said, "but this is a picture of how I am always holding you, even when I am apart from you." For the rest of camp, they trundled around the grounds with grins on their faces, carrying their bent and paint-smeared pictures, reminders of their belovedness.

As the girls put the memory boxes back, Corrie reached in, pulled out the picture, and carried it upstairs to her room. She put it on the bulletin board over her bed, where it remains, a reminder, just like this verse, of what is true.

"You who are loved by God," Moses is saying, "settle deeply into the knowledge of his love for you, quieted by his ceaseless care. Let his love be your home. He surrounds you night and day, absorbing your weakness into his strength and shielding you with his strong presence. You are never outside of his loving embrace. Be at peace. Rest. Be still."

A Sheepish Start to the Day

I woke with a start, almost as if shaken, my mind racing. It was two weeks from the kickoff for a conference for which I was the program director, and I was about four weeks out in my preparations.

Racing like Indy cars through my head were one untended detail after another.

Groggy-eyed and anxious, I dropped into the chair where I have my quiet times. After reading from the Psalms, I turned to where I was in my Gospel reading: "And what pity he felt for the crowds that came, because their problems were so great and they didn't know what to do or where to go for help. They were like sheep without a shepherd" (Matt. 9:36 TLB).

That's me, I thought. *Burdened by problems and, not knowing where to turn for help, relying on myself to solve them.*

Leaning back in my chair, I thought about the way a shepherd takes care of a sheep's problems. He calms the sheep with his care and attention. He reassures the sheep by protecting it from harm. He sees that its every need is met. And he leads the sheep in the right way to go. In other words, he makes the sheep's problems his own. Which means the sheep doesn't have the problem anymore.

Now the sheep has a new problem: Will he trust the shepherd, or will he worry and fret and be anxious?

I chose to slide off the weight of my problems—like a blanket of snow sliding off a sunlit roof—and to let the shepherd bear it. Sure, I still had plenty of things to take care of. But I didn't have to carry them. So I could go about them with peace and focus instead of in harried anxiousness.

God invites us to trust him with the things to which he calls us *and* to trust him with the rest (pun intended). Trusting God means renouncing self-reliance, letting go of control, releasing all things into his hands, and resting in him. What is mine is his, and what is not mine is his. When we trust in this way, we live as though God really exists.

Too often and too easily, however, we fall into "functional atheism": professing faith in the risen Lord but living as though God were altogether absent and uninvolved. We approach life as though it were ours to order and sustain each day, acting like creators rather than creatures. Feeling a great weight always to be *doing*, we resent our limits and constantly try to push past them. We act as though our time and our energy were infinite, and—in defiance of who we are as human beings—we try to do it all. Because, after all, *it's all up to me.* Isn't that what Colossians 1:17 says? "In *me* all things hold together"?

If I were to stand at the edge of Central Park at night and a man were to offer to take me across safely, I could respond in one of two ways. I could ask him to tell me his plans: the precise route he would use and what exactly he would do if I were mugged, if I were approached by a drug dealer, if I twisted my ankle in the dark, or if any number of other circumstances happened. My confidence in the man would go only as far as my confidence in his plan and whether it was to my liking. Really, I would not be trusting him at all but, rather, my ability to evaluate his plan.

How tempting it is to relate to God this way: "God, you tell me your plan, and then I'll tell you if it meets my approval. To the extent that it does, I will put my trust in you."

But there's a better way to get across Central Park: instead of finding a *plan* to my liking, I find a *person* I trust—a person whose strength and wisdom and courage, as well as his regard for me, are proven. Into that person's care I can entrust my well-being.

Learning to trust God requires that we move from trusting God's *plan* to trusting God *himself.* The preamble to a poem by Minnie Louise Haskins captures this important distinction:

> And I said to the man who stood at the gate of the year, Give me a light that I may tread safely into the unknown, and he replied, Go out into the darkness and put your hand into the hand of God. That shall be to you better than a light and safer than the known way. So I went forth, and finding the hand of God, trod gladly into the night.[1]

Dwelling between God's Shoulders

A friend of mine, a gentle-spirited physician in our congregation, asked me a question about the Bible as we stood side by side, scooping chicken onto our plates at a farewell party for a friend. "I've been reading Matthew 18, where it says Jesus called a little child to himself and then said to the disciples, 'I tell you the truth, unless you change and become like this little child, you will never enter the kingdom of heaven. Therefore, whoever humbles himself like this child is the greatest in the kingdom of heaven.'" He looked up from his plate. "What do you think that means?"

I'd often thought about that passage. Which aspect of child-likeness are we to emulate? Freedom? Trust? Present-mindedness? Acceptance? Here was the new and obvious insight that came to me as we talked. We don't have to guess which childlike quality Jesus had in mind. The text spells it out for us: we are to become *humble* like a child.

The fundamental sin in Scripture is self-reliance. The biblical word for it is *pride*. The fundamental virtue in Scripture is God-dependence. The biblical word for it is *humility*.

Think of how a child negotiates life. We had the delight of befriending a couple with twins, two little girls whom we got to know from the first hours after their birth. When I held Gabrielle or Sophia, neither was distracted by how the day would unfold, or burdened by where her food would come from, or preoccupied with who would protect her at night. And as they grew, they remained unguarded and utterly at ease, plunking in my lap to enjoy a book, or climbing on me and grabbing my nose, or nestling into my neck and laughing with no thought beyond the joy of the moment.

Scripture upends so many of the self-evident truths on which we fashion our lives. It turns out that the pride of an adult, which comes of feeling sure it is all up to us (and that we are fully up to the task), breeds anxious, childish scrambling. The humility of a child, who knows that it is all beyond him, is the far more mature response and unleashes peace and freedom.

I recently was stewing over unsettling tectonic shifts that were taking place at work. Everything forward seemed cloudy and uncertain. I felt pressure to solve it all. I needed time with the Lord to extract from him a solution to my quandaries. I settled into my outdoor rocking chair, closed my eyes, and turned to the Lord, quoting Psalm 143:8: "Let me hear of your unfailing love each morning, for I am trusting you" (NLT).

The buzz of a mosquito near my ear prompted me to stop and open the little mailbox next to my chair, in which I keep citronella candles. Out tumbled a pile of twenty-five or thirty three-by-five cards on which my little neighbor friends, Audrey, Avery, and Aiden, had jotted notes and drawn shapes and squiggles. Among them were cards containing one word written in a child's diligent hand: *love*.

"Let me hear word of your love," indeed! You can imagine the grin on my face. I marveled at God's timing—his prompting those exuberant little children to write me notes days before, knowing that this would be the very moment they would tumble out.

It dawned on me that God was inviting me to a like response now: to unfurrow my brow, loosen my grip, abandon my reflex to take matters into my own hands, and adopt instead the simple response of a child's trust, resting in the confidence that all things were already squarely within God's hands.

The happily-ever-after outcome would seem silly, were it not true. I quit trying to take charge of all things and bring them under my mastery. Throughout the remainder of the day, my heart in deep peace, I watched as God went before me into one meeting after another, bringing understanding and unity and wisdom and insight unsought. I just watched and grinned. Why do I always make things so complicated?

179

Erwin Goedicke, my friend and brother in Christ, shared this journal entry with me:

> There are two things I find myself wanting more and more of in my life: more time and more stillness. Not more years, but more unhurried moments that have the feel of eternity in them; moments when nothing else is quite so interesting or compelling or delightful as what is happening in that moment. God-soaked moments. And stillness—the quiet that allows me to become aware of all the sounds and motions and then allows me to find in the midst of them a place even more still to be able to hear God's voice, God's Word. Lord, I ask for that.[2]

Our hearts are restless, O Lord, until they rest in you.

15

The Beautiful Life

There is always time enough in a day to do God's will.

Roy Lessin, *Meet Me in the Meadow*

Though I am always in haste, I am never in a hurry, because I never undertake any more work than I can go through with perfect calmness of spirit.

John Wesley, letter to Mrs. Emma Moon

John Wesley's conversation is good, but he is never at leisure. He is always obliged to go at a certain hour. This is very disagreeable to a man who loves to fold his legs and have his talk out as I do.

Samuel Johnson, in conversation with James Boswell

Harmony, balance, and rhythm. . . . Without them civilization is out of whack.

George Yeoman Pocock

The spirit of Joy and the spirit of Hurry cannot live in the same house. Joy, not Hurry, is an earnest of the presence of God.

Evelyn Underhill, *Concerning the Inner Life with the House of the Soul*

He has made everything beautiful in its time.

Ecclesiastes 3:11

Walla, walla, walla, wah-gunk, wah-gunk, wah-gunk. Click. I'd done it again.

I was on my way past our little laundry room when it occurred to me that it might be helpful to run a quick load. But when I tugged on the door of our clothes chute overhead, it spewed out a multicolored stream of sleeves and pockets and cuffs and collars that mounded knee-high on the floor at my feet.

Fourteen things more important than laundry competed for my attention as I grumpily sorted the clothes. "Light, quiet time, light, dark, white, cut the grass, white, balance the checkbook, call for a dishwasher repairman, colors, dark, date time with kids, white, call my sister, light . . ."

I grabbed the biggest pile and stuffed the washing machine to the brim. When the machine got to the spin cycle, it began to sound like a bighorn sheep butting a VW bus. The whole end of the house was shaking before the machine finally lurched to a stop.

The washing machine was too full and out of balance. So it shut down until the weight got redistributed and it could properly finish its task. The repairman called it "tilting."

"Out of order" is as apt a description of an overloaded and out-of-balance life as of a stuffed and lopsided washing machine. How nice it would be if attaining the grail-like ideal of a balanced life were as easy as rearranging a few dripping towels. But life, with all its dynamism and complexity, resists tidy solutions. Balance is elusive. Real life seems to conspire against its own graceful expression.

Inelegant Living

Artists will tell you that composition—how you arrange the elements in a painting—is as important as the subject itself. Laid out in one way, the elements can be crowded and chaotic, more jarring than pleasing. But the same elements arranged differently can be soothing and inviting. Harmony and proportion contribute to what we find pleasing.

Have you ever been in an art gallery and rounded the corner from the Impressionists to the Modernists? The effect is striking—and meant to be. While there are many words I would use to describe modern art—evocative, jarring, arresting, thought-provoking—*elegant* is not usually among them.

It intrigues me how often our contemporary lives look like contemporary art pieces.

Sometimes, like an Yves Klein canvas painted entirely of a single color, my life is a picture of being bent on one thing. Consumed by the immediacy of what is before me and forgetting all else, I allow a conversation to carry halfway through my next appointment or I work right through dinner. Not only in any given day but also across larger swaths of time, I can let one thing dominate my attention, to the neglect of the many other responsibilities that also require tending. No elegance in that.

Other times, like a Jackson Pollock canvas bestrewn with paint splatters, my life is a picture of jumping chaotically from thing to thing. This tends to happen after a bent-on-one-thing season: I realize I've got twenty other things I should have been focusing on as well. Then, in one of my least effective (and least attractive) modes, I leap about, trying to do it all, anxious about everything and doing nothing well.

There is an art to crafting our lives in the day to day. God calls us to lives fashioned of the things that matter most woven into a pleasing whole. Three compositional elements, balance, rhythm, and margin, are of particular importance in the elegant ordering of our days:

balance: incorporating the right elements in the right proportion

rhythm: moving wisely and gracefully between those elements over time margin: taking ample time in and around those elements for reflection, prayer, and perspective

Balance Statement

At first glance, balance seems to be the key to a less hurried and more sane life. Sebastian Junger describes poignantly the cost of imbalance in his unsettling book *The Perfect Storm*. The relevance of his description of an overloaded ship is obvious.

> Two forces are locked in combat for a ship: the downward push of gravity and the upward lift of buoyancy. Gravity is the combined weight of the vessel and everything on it—crew, cargo, fishing gear—seeking the center of the earth. Buoyancy is the force of all the enclosed air in the hull trying to rise above water level.
>
> On a trim and stable ship, these two forces are equal and cancel each other out along the centerline; but all this changes when a boat gets shoved over on her side. . . .
>
> She winds up one way or another in a position from which she cannot recover. Among marine architects this is known as the *zero-moment point*—the point of no return. The transition from crisis to catastrophe is fast, probably less than a minute.[1]

It would be tempting to conclude that staying afloat in life comes down to one thing: how much is stacked on our decks. But what matters more than overload is balance—avoiding that zero-moment point and so staying out of the drink.

How to find that elusive balance? One approach offers formulas to help us determine how our time should be rightly divided. For example, Gale Sayers's autobiography, *I Am Third*, captures in its title the priorities by which he sought to live: "The Lord is first, my friends are second, and I am third."[2] A familiar variation on this theme is the JOY motto: Jesus, others, you.

The advantage of these approaches is that they press us to reflect on our decisions rather than making them unthinkingly. They can jar us out of our default mode of putting ourselves first or of always saying yes to more.

One disadvantage, though, is that the guidance they offer is not always clear. Do I rotate through the three as if I were dealing cards: God, others, self, God, others, self? Or do I exhaust one completely before I take up the next, doing everything I can to serve God before giving a thought to my neighbor, which could lead me into monkish remove? And the categories are not as mutually exclusive as they seem. Don't I serve God when I serve my neighbor? Don't I meet my own needs when I worship God or find a way to help someone in need?

There is another deeper concern. Formulas inadvertently make mechanical what God intends to be personal. While God is the obvious place to start, "God first" can treat God as a thing to do rather than as a King whose voice we hear and obey. Spirit-led living is replaced by priority-driven living.

It is better, I think, to frame our approach in terms of first allegiance and lesser allegiances. In seeking life balance, the crucial bedrock question is not to *which priorities* we yield but to *whose will* we yield—not *the things of God come ahead of the things of me* but rather *God's will comes ahead of mine.* Or, said another way, we let the captain decide what goes on board.

Balance is not the product of calculation—forty-three minutes talking with my wife, nine hours and four minutes doing ministry, seventeen minutes with each of my kids, fourteen minutes reading each day—but of closeness with God. Balance is not the working out of a formula but the outworking of faith, of obedient confidence in God as he directs us. As C. S. Lewis says, "The real question is, which (when the alternative comes) do you serve, or choose, or put first? To which claim does your will, in the last resort, yield?"[3] Balance is art, not painting by the numbers. But I am not the ultimate artist. God is. I'm but the canvas. We know this intuitively. That what-is-it-about-you quality we sense in someone whose life is surrendered to God is not of their doing. That is elegance of God's making.

It is up to God to determine the right elements in our lives and to direct us in their right proportion. But there is more to elegance than simply having the right pieces in a composition.

Rhythm Instrument

Balance is a moment-in-time word for something that in reality is much more dynamic. In daily life, we experience something closer to rhythm, which is balance over time.

Every New Year's Eve as I was growing up, our family went to the Millers' house, where we kids played in a kid-heaven basement for hours. Pool table, Ping-Pong table, Hula-hoops, Shoot the Moon, Labyrinth, playground balls, dartboard, board games, mattresses to leap on—all treasures calculated to delight a child's heart.

Inevitably, at some point in the evening, like Charlie Brown carrying his football back to Lucy, I would make my way over to that exasperating torture device, the balance board, consisting of a plank laid across a wooden cylinder. The goal was to place one foot on each end of the board and try to position your body in such a way that you were balanced on the cylinder.

I would plant one foot on each end of the tilted board, cant my weight out over the raised end, and—swoosh—the cylinder would roll, the board would sail right past the balance point, and I'd land with a thud on the other end. Trying again, I'd end up right where I started, flying past the balance point like it was an oasis on the Chicago tollway. Only now do I realize that, in spite of its name, the goal of the balance board was *rhythm*, not balance—rocking back and forth like a slalom skier in a sustained and dynamic motion.

So too in life. In any given moment, life is out of balance, and it always will be. We are always falling into or out of something. However much we may wish to deny it, we are all one-thing-at-a-time sorts of people in a lots-to-get-done sort of world.

I had a fascinating conversation with a professor of physiology who explained that almost every human function is rhythmic: the beating of the heart and pulsing of blood, the intake and expulsion of air, the compressing and relaxing of the gastrointestinal tract, the tightening and loosening of muscles as we work, the falling and catching of our bodies with each stride as we walk, even the circadian rhythms that govern our sleep and sense of time. For a human being, he said, a state of balance means death. *Homeostasis* is a misleading description of human health; *homeodynamics* is more accurate.

He then pointed out something I'd never noticed, in spite of the roughly 275 million breaths I've taken in my lifetime: when we breathe, we don't follow a strict balance of in and out. We actually breathe in, breathe out, and then pause. We breathe asymmetrically.

Symmetry, a perfect matching and evenness of all elements, is a classic formula for composition in painting or architecture in which every element has its mirror. It is the picture of balance. But while symmetry can be appealing to look at, it can be unsatisfying to live in, feeling stiff, sterile, and less than human. (Think, for instance, of the stiff formality of the Parthenon in Athens or Versailles near Paris.)

Often, the most appealing sort of balance in composition is the product of artful *asymmetry*. In art, this can take many forms: one element in focus and the others blurry, a single larger element on one side offset by two or more smaller elements on the other, a predominance of dark countered by an angled shaft of light, subjects arrayed on a dynamic angle rather than squarely situated front and center. Think of Frank Lloyd Wright's brilliantly jumbled house Falling Water.

We all know those who are so strict in their apportionment of time, so rigorous in their plans and commitments, that they are as stiff and symmetrical as a formal dining room. But the goal with our use of time is not to get everything precisely even, equal bits going here and there. Rather, as we seek God and follow him into his will for us, we allow him to make "ordinate" or rightly proportioned our respective commitments. As he prompts us, we place the weight of our attention first here, then over there, now back here, then over there, less time here, more there, in a manner that arrives at an elegant equilibrium and balance over time.

At times, the right rhythm in my life means a disproportionate amount of my time goes to my occupation, at considerable cost to my family. For a long season, our church was engaged in the time-swallowing process of discerning whether we should change denominations. The process was demanding beyond description, requiring the investment of hundreds of hours. Little did we know that it would be *three years* before the process was completed.

My marriage and my ministry should have taken serious hits. But God gave me what I needed, what we lacked, what the circumstances required. Though I experienced little balance during that time, God met me—met us. Just as Philippians 4:19 promises, "My God will meet all your needs according to the riches of his glory in Christ Jesus."

At other times, a rightly ordered life means a disproportionate amount of my time goes to my family, at cost to my work. One of our children had a medical issue at one point that required an investment of considerable time for meetings with advisors and appointments with doctors—to all of which it was right for me to give myself. At another point, a child got married. In the days leading up to that event, a disproportionate amount of my time rightly went to those joyful preparations.

At still other times, the life to which I'm called looks remarkably self-centered, and ministry and family both go by the wayside. For example, a couple of times a year, I spend a day with a dear friend of the soul. We walk along Lake Michigan or sit on a porch in the rain, opening the deep recesses of our hearts to one another and seeking the Lord together. Other times, I head off alone to a cabin for a day to rest and plan and pray. At still others, I gather with a delightful group of thinkers, and we share bits we've been writing. These are things into which I believe God calls me, but they pull me away from work and the home front.

It sounds simplistic, but I don't know a better way to find balance over time than to pray. Artful rhythm comes as the answer to familiar prayers such as those in the Psalms. (In chapter 12, I described how I let the words of Psalm 143:8–11 guide my praying.) My experience is that when I am faithful to ask, God is faithful to answer. He brings perspective, clarifies priorities, doles out insight, and points out missteps and next steps.

Rhythm and balance are the outworking of attentiveness to God over time, not a formulaic symmetry forced upon the various pieces of our lives. It is the led life. To what, Lord, would you have me give my time and energy now? And now?

Alongside balance and rhythm, one other crucial and often overlooked element contributes to elegance in a composition: margin.

Margin Notes

When Native Americans canoed along the Wabash River two hundred years ago, 85 percent of Indiana was covered with lush, old-growth forest. Then settlers began to push their way into the state in the 1800s. Discovering how rich and fertile was the soil, they quickly cleared land for farming. Today, only 15 percent of the state remains wooded.

For nearly two hundred years, a farmer's standard approach was to clear a field of its trees and shrubs and grassland right up to the river banks. In the short run, he planted more seed, grew more crops, and made more money. But the long run was a different story. Without some sort of grass margin or tree buffer between the rows of corn and the banks of the river—environmentalists call them filter strips—storm runoff and flooding began to rob the farmer of his precious topsoil, ruining both the river and his farmland.

As in farming, so in life. If we fill every minute of time we've got with activity, we set ourselves up for an erosion of energy and effectiveness that can potentially lead to failure.

Robert Murray M'Cheyne, a gifted Scottish preacher, died at age twenty-nine. Ruing the deadly cost of his overwork and constant busyness, he is said to have lamented on his deathbed, "The Lord gave me a horse to ride and a message to deliver. Alas, I have killed the horse and can no longer deliver the message."

Shifting metaphors from agriculture to architecture, when new buildings are erected, fire codes require that reinforced doors be installed at key locations to keep fires from spreading. Fire doors are rated by what are called *minutes integrity*. Depending on the composition of a door and its seals, the door might be rated an FD30 or an FD60, meaning it is able to withstand extreme temperatures for at least that number of minutes.

This offers another fascinating way of thinking about margin. When I find myself facing the heat of adverse circumstances, how many minutes integrity do I have? How long before I am smoldering with impatience, burning up with anger, or melting down in despair? The decisions I make about the time I spend *between* commitments will have everything to do with how well I withstand the heat in the midst of them.

Burnout is not a time-management problem. It's not a failure to plan. Burnout is ultimately a failure of margin. It is the inelegant insanity of filling every inch of canvas with activity.

I'm not advocating that, out of a paradigm of scarcity and fear, we stockpile our time for ourselves and make available only a modicum of time and effort for others. Time-greed and miserliness have no place in the kingdom. God calls us to give ourselves to the things of God. But that doesn't mean filling every moment from waking to sleeping with activity. To sustain a life of fruitful service for the long haul, we must cultivate margin. We have to learn how to finish before we're finished.

What exactly does margin look like? Here are some ways I have sought to cultivate it. Occasionally on my way to work, I will turn right at the end of our street instead of left, taking a few extra minutes to enjoy the tapestry of the morning skies before heading in to the office. On the way home from a stressful meeting, I've been known to stop at a roadside park, pull out the backpacker's chair in my trunk, and read for a few minutes. In the crunch of ministry-related demands, I'll call a soul friend as I drive between meetings and ask for prayer.

Sometimes between appointments, I walk out onto our church grounds and enjoy the beauty or just close the door to my office and take a deep breath. I have a note over my desk that says, "Look up." Between appointments, I try to take a moment to give God thanks for how he met me in whatever I just finished and ask him to meet me in whatever I'm about to start.

Margin requires deciding when the day is done. Electricity tempts us to stretch the day into the night. So does our never-ending to-do list. But there will always be more to do. Sharon and I try to call it a day at 9:30 or 10 to have a bit of margin for reading and connecting before bed. In effect, we are saying, "Enough. We've done the work of the day. Tomorrow has its own worries. Let's entrust these things to God, get some good sleep, and resume—as he leads us—tomorrow."

Deciding ahead of time on a reasonable workweek is another way to achieve a bit of margin. With Sharon, I try prayerfully to arrive at a workable work schedule for me, and I try hard to honor it. We may adjust it during different seasons of life, based on our family needs and my ministry demands. I also try to limit my evening commitments to two a week and to honor my days off and take my vacation days.

When work takes me out of town, I try to map out a nearby place I can visit for a quick adventure amid the demands of days and nights filled with meetings: sunrise at Canaveral National Seashore near Orlando, sunset on Cannon Beach outside Portland, hiking Mount Cutler near Colorado Springs. And once a year, I spend four days with a group of twelve other pastors to replenish my soul and recalibrate for the demands of ministry.

Margin means a buffer of energy, not just time. When I played tennis as a teenager, my serves were erratic. I'd try to hit every ball as hard as I could, and for every one that went into the court, three others sailed into the net, over the back fence, into the adjoining court. My mom got me a few lessons, and my instructor told me to ease off on my serve and to try hitting the ball at about 95 percent. It made no sense to me. But to my surprise and delight, I found myself serving more consistently and every bit as hard.

I try to apply that same principle to the way I work. Rather than giving 100 percent to whatever or whoever is before me, I try to ease back just a bit and give 95 percent of myself, holding just the smallest part of myself in reserve. Not only am I more efficient and effective at work, and every bit as present to the individuals or projects before me, but that reserve accumulates, and when I get home at the end of the day, I give my wife and kids not an emptied husk of a man but a husband and father with energy to jump in, be present, listen, and serve.

Margin also brings needed perspective to our lives. One of my favorite adventure stories is the true tale of Ernest Shackleton rescuing his crew from a failed Antarctic expedition, recounted masterfully by Alfred Lansing in his book *Endurance*. At one point,

Shackleton and a handful of others jury-rigged a twenty-two-foot
lifeboat and sailed eight hundred miles across some of the stormi-
est seas on the planet, aiming for South Georgia Island, a bump of
rock the size of a postage stamp. If they missed, there was nothing
but more water for thousands of miles. They and the entire crew
would be lost. Their lives hung on hitting the mark, and everything
seemed to conspire against their doing so. They faced seas strewn
with ice blocks, gale-force winds, icing rain, and fifty-foot waves.

Only four times in those seventeen days did breaks in the cloud
cover allow Frank Worsley, the ship's captain, to stick his head out
from under the tarp, point his sextant toward the bobbing sun, and
take a quick read. He got his bearing as best he could and adjusted
their trajectory accordingly. Miraculously, they hit the island dead
on. Seafarers who hear the story still shake their heads in wonder.

We have to stop and get our bearings too. When my nose is
six inches off my desk, I can see only the thing right before me,
and I live accordingly, myopically. Only as I lean back from my
life can I see it for what it is. Better still, when I get up and walk
away and look back at it from the other side of the room, I begin
to see its beauties and its inelegancies—to see my life as God sees
it and adjust accordingly. Margin is space along the edge of our
lives into which we can step and get our bearings again, ensuring
that we are on course and giving us room to make whatever course
corrections are necessary.

Our morning devotional times have this sort of perspectival
dimension, as we invite God to order our activities before we find
ourselves in the thick of them. Margin at the end of the day can
have an equally salubrious effect. Our fathers in the faith advocated
a nightly spiritual discipline called the *examen*, in which we look
back across the day and ask God to lend us his perspective. Francis
de Sales, in his *Introduction to the Devout Life*, suggests reviewing
the day with gratitude, looking first for evidence of God's care
throughout. Then we reflect on our own doings. In those places

where we have done good, we give God thanks; in those where we have fallen short and done wrong, we confess them and ask for God's forgiveness. In this way, we invite God to align our view of our lives with his and to change course accordingly.[4]

Margin can be found all along the daily meandering of time, not just at the start and end of the day. I've long appreciated the daily pattern that Psalm 110 suggests. In verse 3, it says, "Your strength will be renewed each day like the morning dew," and then in verse 7, "He himself will be refreshed from brooks along the way" (NLT). Begin the day by drinking deeply of God, and then, busy or not, return to him often for replenishment throughout the day.

As with balance and rhythm, artful living is impossible without margin for reflection. Lacking time to reflect, we don't live; we merely react. We don't do what we're truly called to do but only what is next, or closest, or easiest, or most urgent, or most appealing. We live by reflex, not by reflection.

For something to be beautiful, it needs breathing room. An artist needs to be as willing to leave out as to leave in. In his rich book on music and time, Jeremy Begbie reminds us that pianist Arthur Schnabel once said, "The pauses between the notes—ah, that is where the art resides."[5] Beauty is found in the in-between spaces—in the resonant pause between notes, the gathered stillness before a *grand jeté*, or the space between figures in a painting.

~~~

After a masterful dance, concert, or film, as we gather our coats and head for the doors, we're not likely to turn to one another and say, "Well, they got it done."

So much of time management is about getting to stuff and getting through stuff. But life is measured by more than accomplishment. God-led balance, rhythm, and margin infuse our lives with God-given beauty, and that beauty is part of the very fruit he means to bear in and through us.

16

Still Life

Life is not an emergency.
Ann Voskamp,
A Holy Experience blog

Making haste is not a moral obligation.
Ralph Keyes, *Timelock*

Work is not always required. . . . There is such a thing as sacred idleness, the cultivation of which is now fearfully neglected.
George MacDonald

Blessed be the God of love,
Who gave me eyes, and light, and power this day,
Both to be busie, and to play.
George Herbert, "Even-song"

It's okay to have a busy life. It's crazy to have a busy soul.
Paul Miller, *A Praying Life*

What was created on the seventh day? Tranquility.
Genesis Rabba 10:9

The day was crisp, the sun sparkling off the thick blanket of snow, the chill tingling my cheeks. I padded through twelve inches of unspoiled white that had fallen the day before, my snowshoes leaving the only prints in the valley. What is so satisfying about being the first to plant footprints in the snow? Across the meadow, into the woods, toward the ridge that looked over the river, I whumped my way.

Suddenly, I stopped. I wasn't the first one here after all. In front of me were odd tracks—a long, narrow chute of packed snow.

I went twenty feet more and stopped. The snow chute ended. In its place was a line of paired puncture points wending through the trees. I went another twenty feet, and the chute picked up again. Looking closer, I saw what appeared to be the entry points of small ski poles every few feet alongside the snow channel. Looking closer still, I saw they had been made by feet—feet too small and too far apart to be human. As I neared the river's edge, I saw another chute, this one a sliding S shape that ran right down into the river.

It finally dawned on me. This was an otter track! When I got home, I consulted a book by Paul Rezendes: "When otters move on snow they tend to bound a few steps, then get down on their belly and slide, pushing themselves along with their short legs as though they were swimming. . . . Often an otter slide will lead down a hill and straight into water."[1]

Bound, slide, bound, slide. Work, rest, work, rest. That's how we "otter" live our lives.

Tired Out

We are prone to believe that rest should come only after everything else is finished. In Acts 13:36, we read, "When David had served God's purpose in his own generation, he fell asleep." It sounds like he stayed up until he got it all done!

But there is a rest that we can enjoy even while much remains to be done. Until the Lord returns, all completions are only provisional completions anyway. This side of the grave, we will only ever experience things being partway done.

When we first arrived in the Colorado Rockies for a vacation a few years ago, I hopped on my bike and sped up a mountain path. Later, stopping to catch my breath in the high altitude, I sat next to a mountain stream. The water—snowmelt clear and cold—raced past, rushing around boulders, plummeting over logs, swirling and frothing. I could hear a range of pitches: the high notes of splashing drops and roiling waves; the midrange slurping and gurgling of hydraulics; the deep, thunder-like collision of current with mountain. All was a rush of noise and motion.

Yet right in front of me was stillness. To either side of two substantial boulders, the current rippled and raced, but here it gathered into a smooth calm. Then, after a spell, the water in the eddy reentered the torrent and sped downstream.

As we weary humans negotiate the currents of time, God has provided places of pause and rest for us. Sleep and Sabbath—*shennat* and *shabbat*, as we encounter them in the Hebrew text—are two God-given eddies in the fast-rushing river of time.

Sleep: The Daily Gift

I still remember the odd and unpleasant sensation of waking up to find myself standing in front of my congregation. I was the father of four young children, including a newborn, and I had been pushing to wrap up my doctoral thesis. I was so tired that I had fallen asleep during a pause while I was praying before my sermon. As Uncle Remus put it, "Ole man Nod wuz ridin' on my eyeleds."[2]

God calls his people to rhythms of work and rest. The most obvious of these, though perhaps the most often denied, is nightly sleep.

I don't know how many times over the years I've heard my kids say, "But, Daddy, I don't *want* to go to bed! I'm not even *tired*!" Meanwhile, their eyes are drooping, and their yawns are the size of Mammoth Cave.

We adults are worse than our kids. We overschedule our days, denying the limits of our time and energy, and inevitably leave for ourselves miles to walk and mounds to sort before we sleep. Whatever we can do to push sleep away and extend our productive moments we will do. In her book *The Secret Life of Sleep*, Kat Duff diagnoses us as "enamored with wakefulness."[3]

One way we extend the day is to push back the darkness. Artificial light has greatly blessed our world; late-night truck drivers and nightshift ER docs especially have reason to be grateful. But Thomas Edison's bright creation has a dark side. No longer is there a clear dividing line between day and night, making it harder and harder to call it a day.

We postpone sleep by injecting our bodies with weariness-deferring ingredients of the sort we find in coffee, tea, chocolate, soda, and energy drinks. (A sign behind the counter at a local ice-cream shop says, "DRINK COFFEE: Do stupid things faster with more energy.") On the other end of the night, morning bullies its way into our shortened sleep with the jarring ringing of alarm clocks. Sugar and caffeine intake props us up for a new day. Several people I know can't begin the day without being galvanized into action by the 9 tablespoons of sugar and the 140 grams of caffeine found in a can of Mountain Dew.

Now there's Provigil, a drug that takes away the need for sleep, developed to help those with narcolepsy and other sleep disorders. A vast underground Provigil market exists for those who simply want to function with *less* sleep. According to Duff, this drug can keep people awake and alert for two days "without the jitters of caffeine, the mood swings of amphetamines, or sleep-debt accumulation." Even though scientists aren't sure how the drug works, don't know if it's addictive, and are uncertain about long-term effects, sales are well over $1 billion a year.[4]

We are more likely to see sleep as an annoyance, a disruption, or a concession than as a gift. But Scripture presses a different view. For the first man and woman, the first part of the first day was not the day at all. It was night. After God created humanity, we're told, "God saw all that he had made, and it was very good. And there was *evening*, and there was morning—the sixth day" (Gen. 1:31, italics added). God created man and woman, tucked them in bed, and wished them good night.

I love the way John Milton in *Paradise Lost* envisions that moment when Adam and Eve stand under the starry sky for the first time. They say:

> Thou also mad'st the night,
> Maker Omnipotent, and thou the day.
> . . . [We] shall extol
> Thy goodness infinite, both when we wake,
> And when we seek, as now, thy gift of sleep.[5]

We plop our heads on our pillows and grumble and complain, but God desires of us a very different sort of perspective—to see sleep as a grace gift:

> In peace I will lie down and sleep,
> for you alone, LORD, make me dwell in safety. (Ps. 4:8)

> Let them sing for joy as they lie on their beds. (Ps. 149:5 NLT)

Sleep sings of the goodness and glory of God—how the Creator loves his creatures, replenishing them night after night, infusing them with vigor and new life, equipping them for each day.

God could have made us to need less sleep. He could have instructed our melatonins to kick in with a little more rigor and made our metabolism more efficient so that we could run for days on end. But he didn't, and (try as we might) we can't.

It almost looks as if God *designed* us to need sleep. A lot of sleep. Right from the start, even before Adam and Eve's rebellion, God designed us to have to cease our activity, lie down, and surrender ourselves into vulnerability, inactivity, unproductivity.

I believe God's gift of sleep goes beyond mere physical replenishment. It is also an opportunity for *relinquishment*. Eugene Peterson reminds us, "This Hebrew evening/morning sequence conditions us to the rhythms of grace. . . . Evening: God begins, without our help, his creative day. Morning: God calls us to enjoy and share and develop the work he initiated."[6]

Sleep is an admission of our creaturely limits and a confession that we are more than the sum of the tasks on our to-do list. The *New Zealand Prayer Book* suggests a night prayer that includes these lines: "Lord, it is night after a long day. What has been done has been done; what has not been done has not been done. Let it be. . . . The night heralds the dawn. Let us look expectantly to a new day, new joys, new possibilities."[7]

Sleep proclaims our moment-by-moment dependency upon God. How vulnerable we are as we slumber, a breath away from death but for God's watchful care and provision. Medieval Christians saw the resemblance between sleep and death and encouraged believers to see the one as a rehearsal for the other. The familiar, thousand-year-old child's prayer reflects this: "Now I lay me down to sleep, I pray the Lord my soul to keep. If I should die before I wake, I pray the Lord my soul to take." Each time we sleep, we say, "God, my life is in your hands."

A few weeks ago, I got to be the first sitter for one-week-old Julia, the adorable firstborn of dear and trusting friends. I spent the entire evening with her asleep on my chest, her gentle breaths like whispers of peace, and I couldn't stop grinning. What a picture of trust was this child slumbering in my arms, cooing with confidence in my care. Her relaxed sleep said, "I relinquish myself utterly into your safekeeping."

When we acknowledge our creaturely limits, we glorify our Creator. When we sleep, we say, "I am not God, but God is. Glory be to his name!"

For several years now, believing that God gives me both my need for sleep and sufficient time to accomplish the things to which he calls me when I am awake, I have gone to bed sufficiently early (most nights) so I can sleep until my body wakes itself, refreshed for the day. It may be that God would have us rethink our time use if we find we need to rely on an alarm or a cup of coffee too often to rouse ourselves from sleep.

Into the Fold

In Ireland, God gave me a personal parable about his gift of sleep. On the first day of my trip, I drove from Giant's Causeway on the far northeast tip of Ireland to the tiny Atlantic town of Portmagee in the southwest corner—in fifteen hours, through the night.

Why the hurry? I was trying to catch a fishing boat to the ancient island monastery of Skellig Michael, and the last boat left port before noon. So I drove until 2:30 in the morning, slept four hours in my car in a church parking lot, and then was on my way again, racing along the winding Irish roads.

When I got to the fishing boat with just minutes to spare, the pilot, a woolly headed, joyful man named Cavanaugh, said, "Ye moost 'ave bun drrrivin like a rrravin' loonatic!" Indeed.

That night, after a full day of ocean going and island scrambling, I retraced my path toward Dublin, where my flight would go out the next morning. After debating whether to squeeze in one more side venture, I conceded my growing weariness and stopped at a bed and breakfast in Bird Hill. A frumpy, smiling older woman greeted me at the door in her "wellies" (rubber boots), fresh from having fed her sheep.

She welcomed me in, tending to me as another of her sheep. When she looked over my shoulder and saw my soggy clothes spread across the backseat of my car, she remarked that I was "in need of a wife, or, short of that, a mother." After throwing my wet clothes in her dryer, she got me settled into my room and expressed her concern that I wake up with sufficient time to get to the airport.

In the morning, I woke to a wonderful breakfast spread in her sunroom—and my clothes folded and neatly stacked by my chair. Just outside the window, sheep lay contentedly or wandered lazily, munching on plentiful grass.

I flipped open my Bible to the next psalm in my reading plan. It was the twenty-third:

> The LORD is my shepherd. . . .
> > He makes me lie down in green pastures,
> he leads me beside quiet waters,
> > he refreshes my soul. (vv. 1–3)

So he does—if we slow down enough to let him.

Sabbath Rest: The Weekly Gift

Sleep is God's gift. So too is the Sabbath. The first rhythm of rest is the daily cycle of wakefulness and sleep. The second is the weekly cycle of work and rest.

In Deuteronomy 5:12–15, God directs his people to keep a weekly "cease effort" (*shabbat*):

> Observe the Sabbath day by keeping it holy, as the LORD your God has commanded you. Six days you shall labor and do all your work, but the seventh day is a sabbath to the LORD your God. On it you

shall not do any work, neither you, nor your son or daughter, nor your male or female servant, nor your ox, your donkey or any of your animals, nor any foreigner residing in your towns, so that your male and female servants may rest, as you do. Remember that you were slaves in Egypt and that the LORD your God brought you out of there with a mighty hand and an outstretched arm. Therefore the LORD your God has commanded you to observe the Sabbath day.

The idea of observing the Sabbath sounds anachronistic, like something from a Jane Austen novel. Maybe the Sabbath was once practical. But today, in our 24/7/365 world? Could anything be more impractical than taking a whole day to do nothing, especially when we already feel so far behind?

Besides, don't Paul's writings release us from having to keep the Sabbath, at least as a specific day that is set apart? Romans 14:5 says, "One person considers one day more sacred than another; another considers every day alike. Each of them should be fully convinced in their own mind." And there's Colossians 2:16–17, where Paul writes, "Do not let anyone judge you by what you eat or drink, or with regard to a religious festival, a New Moon celebration or a Sabbath day. These are a shadow of the things that were to come; the reality, however, is found in Christ." It couldn't get much clearer than that, could it?

Many in the history of the church have agreed. Augustine, Calvin, and Aquinas all viewed the commandment in a figurative and spiritual sense. But Jesus seemed to assume that the Sabbath was still relevant. When the Pharisees confronted him with what is appropriate to do and not to do on the Sabbath, he didn't say, "Sabbath Shmabbath! You don't have to fuss with that old convention any longer." Instead, he said, "The Sabbath was made for man," and "The Son of Man is Lord even of the Sabbath" (Mark 2:27–28). He affirmed the Sabbath as a day given for our benefit and to serve his ends. These words bear weight.

203

Nowhere does the New Testament explicitly discontinue the observance of the Sabbath. It seems to occupy the same unique status as the other Ten Commandments, which—unlike the ceremonial laws or the civil laws of the Old Testament—endure in their authority into the New Testament as an expression of God's best way to live across place and time.

And a closer look at context suggests that Paul was not dismissing Sabbath keeping but rather challenging the false teachers who required keeping the Old Testament law as a way of being right with God. Paul was attacking a perversion of the Sabbath's significance, not the practice of it.

For years—largely based on those two passages from Paul—I saw the Sabbath as a good suggestion. No longer. While I want to approach this issue with theological modesty, I am increasingly persuaded that—as both a gift to be enjoyed and a command to be obeyed—God intends us to keep the Sabbath.

Three ideas sum up what Scripture teaches it means to be faithful to the day: stop, rest, remember.

Stop

Shabbat means to cease effort. For six days, we expend ourselves at work and at home. (Contrary to Protestant work-ethic champions, "six days you shall labor" is meant to be a description, not a command.) On the seventh, we are to follow God's creation pattern and cease our activity.

When in Genesis it says that God "rested" (2:2), it doesn't mean, of course, that God was tired and took a break. Resting here means stopping; God was finished and stopped his creative work. This is similar to a rest in musical notation: we arrest our playing, pausing for a moment without sounding any note.

In the Old Testament, Sabbath observance began with stopping work (Exod. 20:10), such as construction (Exod. 31:13–17),[8] plowing and harvesting (Exod. 34:21), and commerce (Amos 8:4–6). But the admonition also applied more widely to include routine household chores, such as carrying loads (Jer. 17:21), gathering firewood (Num. 15:32–36), and starting a fire for cooking (Exod. 35:3).

Nowhere are we given a comprehensive list of what is off-limits. But anxious not to dishonor God, the Jewish people created what they called a "hedge," a layer of additional commands with which they surrounded the original. They assumed that if they kept the additional rules, they were sure to keep the original one.

But legalism has a way of multiplying yokes, not removing them. By Jesus's time, teachers of the law had transformed this single commandment into a list of more than fifteen hundred types of work in thirty-nine categories, every one ruled out. Here are a few examples—as well as some of the loopholes that inevitably crept in:

You can't wear false teeth, or pick your fingernails, or put on makeup, or fix up your hair. If a hair band placed in your hair before the Sabbath falls out, you have to leave it out.

You can't throw anything more than four yards, unless a dog happens to catch it.

If your house catches on fire on the Sabbath, you can only save enough food for three meals, plus as many changes of clothes as you can wear at one time.

You can't write more than a single letter of the alphabet, unless you write in the dust or in fruit juice that disappears.[9]

A less-strained understanding of the commandment is offered by Joy Davidman, the brilliant writer who became C. S. Lewis's wife in their later years. She defines work as "all the pursuits we engage in for necessity and not for pleasure"[10]—the day-to-day efforts of earning a living and keeping a house and managing life's demands. Whatever we *have* to do, whatever life burdens us to do, is the focus of this command.

Ruth Haley Barton aptly widens this by implication to include eliminating the things that burden us or cause us worry, such as making major decisions. She also advocates setting aside technology, especially that related to our occupations.[11]

We've been practicing the Sabbath for about fifteen years as a family. Borrowing from the Jewish tradition, we sometimes light a pair of candles at sundown on Saturday night to mark the start of our rest. During the next twenty-four hours, we lay aside the have-to's. We let the yard, the laundry, and the bills go, and we guard against Sunday as a day of shopping. Obviously this requires some planning ahead so the day can be free of work and worry. Sometimes the kids will do homework, but we try to keep that from dominating the day. We also try to limit screen time; video games get put away and the computer stays off.

What if you have a job that requires you to work on Sunday? We can't do without policemen, firemen and emergency response teams, the military, church workers, and those in the medical profession. If yours is an occupation that prevents you from taking Sunday as a Sabbath, find another block of time that works. As a pastor, I work on Sunday mornings, but I have largely been able to keep my Sunday afternoons and evenings free of other obligations, and I often allow my Sabbath rest to carry over into the following morning of my day off.

Setting aside a day free of work becomes an act of faith, as every Sabbath comes as an implicit question from God: Will you trust me? When we observe the Sabbath, we answer, "Yes. I trust you, God, to make up for the time I refrain from working. I trust you to provide for me as I choose not to provide for myself." Certainly this was the point of the unique manna Sabbath exception that God gave his people (Exod. 16:21–30).

The Sabbath commandment is the Creator's promise that he will love and provide for his creatures, that he is the author and finisher of our work. Our Sabbath observance is our profession of faith that he is and that he will.

Rest

There's more to the Sabbath than simply stopping what we normally do or exchanging one manner of work for another. "Observe the Sabbath day . . . so that your male and female servants may *rest*, as you do" (Deut. 5:12, 14, italics added).

"In the tempestuous ocean of time and toil there are islands of stillness where man may enter a harbor and reclaim his dignity," writes Abraham Heschel. "The island is the seventh day, the Sabbath."[12] We cease burdensome obligations not so we can take up other burdensome obligations but so we can exit the ceaseless wind and wave of the rest of the week and come to *rest*.

The Hebrew word for "rest" speaks not merely of the absence of activity but of the presence of peace. It is the rest of a bird hushed to tranquility, an army ordered to cease fire, the body made to relax.

For those of us bent on maximizing our output, the day feels like an intrusion. But the day isn't meant to be a burden. It's a gift. Jesus says the Sabbath was given us for our benefit (Mark 2:27), and Isaiah urges us to "call the Sabbath a delight" (Isa. 58:13).

A delight? Earlier generations may have missed the mark here, such as when the four-hundred-year-old Westminster Confession taught that the Sabbath should exclude recreation. The film *Chariots of Fire* tells the true story of Eric Liddell, the Olympic runner who became a missionary in China. You may remember the scene when Eric comes out of church and a soccer ball bounces in front of him, followed by a jostling and laughing group of boys. He pulls the boys aside, hands back the ball, and says to its owner, "D'ya know wha' day it is, lad?" Implication: stop having fun. They walk away chastened and glum. Perhaps it was this theological misstep of our forebearers that informed H. L. Mencken's definition of Puritanism: "the haunting fear that someone, somewhere, may be happy."[13]

What brings you delight? Replenishes you? Restores your soul? This is the day for it. Time in creation, time with family and friends, time alone. Reading, walking, going to a movie. Snuggling, snoozing, exercising. Gardening, cooking, doing a puzzle. Painting a picture, playing a game, watching sports. I like Marva Dawn's criterion: "Activity that is enjoyable and freeing and not undertaken for the purpose of accomplishment qualifies as acceptable for Sabbath time."[14]

According to Moses, *everybody* in the house is to experience rest (Deut. 5:14). If one person's restorative activities drag the rest of the household into burdensome busyness, it's right to do some rethinking. I have great respect for businesses such as Chick-Fil-A and Hobby Lobby that close their doors on Sunday so their "family" of employees can have the day.

Remember

There's one more layer to the Sabbath.

The Exodus version of the fourth commandment explains where the day originated. But Deuteronomy's version explains *why* the day was given. The Sabbath is tied to redemption, to God's gracious work of rescue: "Remember that you were slaves in Egypt and that the LORD your God brought you out of there with a mighty hand and an outstretched arm. *Therefore* the LORD your God has commanded you to observe the Sabbath day" (Deut. 5:15, italics added). The Sabbath was meant to be a repeated reminder—even a reenactment—of the Israelites' rescue. God's people were slaves for four hundred years, and then he set them free. So each week, in remembrance of that redemption, after having "slaved" for six days, they were set free to rest.

This is why Sabbath observance shifted from Saturday to Sunday for the early church. Just as for Jews each Sabbath is intended to be a little Passover, so for Christians each Sunday is intended to be a little Easter. By observing the day, we rehearse God's claim on the whole of our lives by virtue of his having rescued us through Christ.

We can easily lose our way in the sea of time. The Sabbath is our way of reorienting ourselves in the swiftly passing days. It reminds us that God is in our lives and his heart is our home. It also reminds us that our lives belong to God and we are to live them for him. What could bring deeper replenishment of soul than that?

This weekly remembering spills over to our other days. The Sabbath is a "sold" sign planted in the middle of our calendar. In giving a seventh of our time back to the Lord, we acknowledge that *all* of our time belongs to him. By living the Sabbath "to the Lord," we consecrate not just that day but each day. We return life to its rightful owner.

Wake, sleep. Work, cease.

Both sleep and the Sabbath remind us of our creaturely limits. We are not infinite in our power and ability, but we know One who is.

And when we observe the Sabbath, as when we sleep, our ceasing is a way of celebrating. As we lay down what burdens us and take up what replenishes us, we enjoy and honor the One who is life itself.

17

Deeper Still

There is more to life than increasing its speed.

Mahatma Gandhi

Only when we tarry do we touch the holy.

Rainer Maria Rilke, "This Press of Time"

If people concentrated on the really important things in life, there'd be a shortage of fishing poles.

Doug Larson

Men do mightily wrong themselves when they . . . busy themselves only with pots and cups and things at home, or shops and trades and things in the street; but do not live to God manifesting Himself in all the world.

Thomas Traherne, "Meditation 85," *Centuries of Meditations*

I am well again, I came to life in the cool winds and crystal waters of the mountains.

John Muir, "Letter to Mrs. Carr"

The problem is not entirely in finding . . . the time alone, difficult and necessary as that is. The problem is more how to still the soul in the midst of its activities.

Anne Morrow Lindbergh, *Gift from the Sea*

When I was a teenager, I used to fly with my dad in his Cessna 182, a single-engine, four seater that pilots call the station wagon of airplanes. I remember sitting in the copilot seat next to him feeling a hushed thrill, careful not to touch anything as he walked through the preflight checklist.

In the air, my dad never relaxed, constantly assessing the instruments for altitude, direction, rate of speed; scanning the horizon for other planes, weather, landmarks; radioing for traffic, weather conditions, landing arrangements; adjusting direction, rate of climb, wing attitude. Meanwhile, the throb of the engine and the buffets of the wind were unceasing. All was motion and noise, adjustment and readjustment.

Finally, back on the ground at flight's end, my dad cut the engine, and the plane shuddered to a stop. A sudden welcome quiet replaced the pulsing, thrumming clatter.

Only then, as I popped my ears and stretched my limbs, would I hear the high descending whine of the tiny gyroscope behind the instrument panel. The gyro is part of the cluster of instruments that tells the pilot his attitude, heading, and turn rate. It spins at speeds approaching three thousand revolutions per second, powered by a stream of air created by a vacuum pump. When the engine is shut down, though the airflow stops, the gyroscope continues to spin. And spin. And spin.

As we chocked the wheels and tied down the wings, as we emptied the plane and locked it up, as we gathered our gear off the tarmac and threw it into the car, the gyro continued to whir. Twenty minutes could pass before it finally spun to stillness.

How like us.

Ready for a much-needed retreat, I pull up to my friend's cabin and turn off the car. The hubbub and clatter of my schedule-driven, noise-and-motion life shudder to stillness. Yet the noise and motion within me continue to whir for a long time. "Drat. I forgot to call Tom back. I wonder how Diane's recovery is going. We need to check our calendars for that award banquet next week. I wonder if there's any food here. What should I preach on this summer? I wish I'd gotten the bills paid before I left. I wonder if they have any good movies here. I hope I remembered to pack my devotional stuff. I forgot to bring some music. What's the weather supposed to be like? I wonder if my phone works here. I should really . . ."

Gordon MacDonald tells of an explorer venturing into the African interior, eager to arrive as soon as possible at a distant village. He hires local villagers to carry his supplies, and, under his urging, off they speed into the jungle. The next day, however, the Africans refuse to rise. When asked why, they say they went too fast the first day, and they are waiting for their souls to catch up with their bodies.[1] How many days behind are our tired souls, struggling to catch up?

In her poem "Moonlight," Amy Carmichael prays, "Don't let the hurry chase the quiet from our hearts."[2]

The Third Rhythm

As we explored in the previous chapter, the first rhythm of rest is the daily cycle of wakefulness and sleep. The second is the weekly pattern of work and rest. But there is a crucial third rhythm of rest, one we often neglect: the routine cycle of engagement and disengagement, of forward motion followed by retreat into solitude and silence.

Getting still is a prerequisite to encountering God. "Be still" must come before "and know that I am God" (Ps. 46:10). The more I'm on the move, the more occupied I become with motion itself. We say, "Speak, Lord, your servant is li—" But before we even get to the end of the line, we've already moved out of earshot and on to the next thing.

Along with stillness, silence is crucial to the health of the soul. Cornelius Plantinga Jr. observes, "A loss of silence is as serious as a loss of memory and just as disorienting. Silence is, after all, the natural context from which we listen."[3]

Nothing on the surface of our lives suggests the urgency of spending time away in silence. But urgent it is. Jesus urged his followers, "Come with me by yourselves to a quiet place and get some rest" (Mark 6:31). For just that reason, I determined years ago to take a day each month for solitude and silence. It is beyond my capacity to express what it has meant in my life and ministry to take these regular (or, to be more honest, irregular) retreats.

I can never afford to turn away from the mound of work demands—or so I believe—causing me to be far less consistent in this practice than I desire. But the moment I close my office door behind me and head out of town, God seems to draw nearer. My body eases, my perspective begins to clear, and my soul breathes in. I notice beauty. I sleep deeply. I think unhurriedly. I stop rushing to the other end of my quiet times. I slow enough to think and pray about what I'm reading. Inevitably, I come back from time away with renewed intimacy with God, peace of soul, and clarity of purpose.

For true silence and solitude, we have to leave our electronic devices—our phones, our computers—behind. If we don't, we're merely relocating from one address in the State of Distraction to another. We may as well stay put. As David Brooks writes, "Never being out of touch means never being able to get away."[4]

Charles Spurgeon prescribes just the balm our souls crave: "Quietude, which some men cannot abide because it reveals their inward poverty, is as a palace of cedar to the wise, for along its hallowed courts the King in his beauty deigns to walk."[5]

In solitude and stillness, we are truly enabled to encounter God, to hear clearly the whispered invitings and urgings of the Spirit that are so often drowned out by our busyness.

Creation

We have lost something else in our pursuit of perpetual motion. Most of us, if at all, are only vaguely aware of it, but all of us are the poorer for it.

Seldom do we touch the created world. Ears used to the gentle clatter of computer keys are unaccustomed to the splash of a running stream. Fingers familiar with the curve of a steering wheel find the rough bark of a ponderosa pine harsh and unwelcoming. And feet in the habit of strolls on thickly padded office carpet are unsteady in the overturned earth between long rows of summer corn.

We live in a world of interiors, and only rarely do we have to face the unpleasantness of contact with the exterior world. A quick gust of wind and a few drops of rain send us scurrying for cover.

And yet my consistent experience is that when I venture into the natural world, I experience a reinvigorated sense of wonder and awe of God, a new humility, and a fresh willingness to hear his voice. Psalm 95 sings out this triumphant affirmation:

> The LORD is the great God,
>> the great King above all gods.
> In his hands are the depths of the earth,
>> and the mountain peaks belong to him.
> The sea is his, for he made it,
>> and his hands formed the dry land.
> Come, let us bow down in worship,
>> let us kneel before the LORD our Maker. (vv. 3–6)

This passage is one of hundreds of references to creation that thread through Scripture. How can a theme so present in Scripture be so absent from our lives?

Part of God's purpose in creation is for humanity to study his world and see in it something of him. The created world is a

214

showcase of our Lord's awesome artistry. Paul, in his letter to the Romans, reminds us of this. God's invisible qualities, "his eternal power and divine nature," can be clearly seen and understood from what he has made (1:20). "There's not a plant or flower below but makes Thy glories known," wrote Isaac Watts.[6]

We are out of eyeshot of creation's testimonies, and our grasp of God's might and mystery has atrophied. The transcendence of God, his majestic "otherness," has been all but lost. Lacking the perspective that time in nature brings, we have whittled God down to something less than the glorious One we meet in Scripture.

According to Scripture, because of the glimpses of God that it yields, nature is meant to be an integral, not a peripheral, part of the spiritual life. It is time for us to venture out, to embark on expeditions into God's world as an intentional spiritual practice. Fittingly, the word *expedition* has its origin in a Latin phrase that means "to free someone caught by the foot." We are, many of us, stuck. We live in insulated indoor pockets tucked away from the marvelous handiwork of God, and we desperately need to get out.

Twice in the early chapters of Luke, we're told that Jesus, at key junctures in his ministry, ventured out. One time, after an all-night meeting of healing and exorcism in Capernaum, "at daybreak Jesus went out to a solitary place" (Luke 4:42). When the crowds finally tracked him down, his reply reflected new—or renewed—perspective. He reminded them that he was called not just to those in front of him but to others as well.

Shortly after that, Jesus spent an entire night on a mountainside to pray. The reason? To discern those into whom he would pour himself during the next three years of ministry. Jesus's example is not just of prayer but of heading out into creation to hear his Father's quiet words.

A good friend in our home group wrote me a letter some time back to remind me of this. Knowing as she did how much I enjoy the outdoors, she pointed out this unique aspect of Jesus's relationship with the Father—venturing outside to pray—and encouraged me to do the same.

How could I do that? I grew up in the United States, where "in" is work and "out" is play. How could I venture out and still take myself seriously?

But my friend's words have continued to gently prod me. As often as I can, I have my quiet times somewhere other than indoors, and my devotional life has been transformed as a result. Dozens of journal entries and poems reflect the way that my soul has been made more attentive to the words and ways of God by settling in among his works and pondering them. The psalmist says, "Great are the works of the LORD, studied by all who delight in them" (Ps. 111:2 ESV). In creation more than in any other setting I experience the powerful presence of the living God.

In addition to having my morning devotional time outside whenever possible, I try to get away once a quarter for at least twenty-four hours alone. Friends have, with astonishing generosity, made their place available for a getaway. I read Scripture and pray and write in my journal. Sometimes I watch a movie or take a nap.

But nonnegotiable in those too-brief hours away is time outside: hiking, canoeing, snowshoeing, dune walking, bird watching, owl calling, animal tracking, wildflower picking, rock hunting, leaf collecting, picture taking. I study the face of the moon, kayak on a lake under a full moon, laze in the sun, sleep under the stars.

When I am in creation, I attend to God's works. I begin to *notice*, distinguishing different types of rocks or birds or trees, learning constellations and features on the face of the moon, paying attention to what animals make which sorts of tracks, what birds shed which sorts of feathers, what trees have which sorts of bark, what weather produces which sorts of clouds.

Paying careful attention to God's works, I cannot help but incline my ear to God's words too. Listening for God's voice is a

216

natural extension of looking for his touch. Venturing into creation fosters wonder at the ways of God and readies me to hear the Spirit's whispered words.

Creation exists, in large part, that we might glimpse the Creator in its every crease and corner. "Divinity is not playful," writes Annie Dillard. "The universe was not made in jest but in solid incomprehensible earnest by a power that is unfathomably secret, and holy, and fleet. There is nothing to be done about it but ignore it or see it."[7] Let's venture out, with eyes made wise to God's purposes and ears attentive to his voice. A world charged with the grandeur of God awaits us.

I love how Elizabeth Barrett Browning expresses the choice before each of us:

> Earth's crammed with heaven,
> And every common bush afire with God;
> But only he who sees, takes off his shoes,
> The rest sit round it and pluck blackberries.[8]

Tranquility

It was 9:30 or so, a midsummer night in the Upper Peninsula of Michigan. The sun, though long since set, left faint traces of pale pink in the western sky, and the air was yet warm. I pushed the canoe into the Tahquamenon and headed upriver.

I was alone, no one within miles, and but for the dripping of water off my paddle between strokes and the faint lap of tiny waves against the prow of the canoe, all was silent and still.

I pressed my way up the slow-moving river toward the beaver lodge I'd seen earlier. I could just make out the outlines of the trees and their reflections along the bank, giant wedges of black receding toward the horizon. Overhead, the stars began to emerge jewel-like: the Big Dipper, Cassiopeia, the North Star. Mars hung red in the east.

I felt as though I were floating in the air and paddling the breeze. The quiet and calm were almost surreal.

Suddenly, to my left, I saw a huge ball of fire dancing between the tree trunks. The splash of light and color was so jarring that I could almost hear it. It took me a minute to realize I was looking at the rising moon, full and dripping gold through the trees.

I quickly paddled to the opposite side of the river and turned, stopped, and stared. The moon's reflection fell on the soft surface of the water and broke into golden bands of light. I could hardly breathe. How do you take in such a thing?

Minutes passed before I moved. Then I dipped paddle into water and continued upriver toward the glow.

As I neared the beaver lodge, I heard a loud tramping in the woods to my right. I turned to investigate. As I neared the shore, the noise stopped. There was a quiet plish, then slow ripples circled out. I looked behind me just in time to see a beaver paddle by, a silent silhouette against the last faint patches of light. Then in a splash of commotion he rose up, smacked his tail against the water in warning, and disappeared. In the quiet of the night, the smack was thunderous.

I paddled back across the river to his den to see if I might catch another glimpse of him. To my delight, I heard the expectant, high-pitched squeals of beaver cubs inside. Then, just to my right, another beaver slapped its tail, and the squeals suddenly fell silent.

Long minutes later, I turned downriver for home. As I arced out into the current, I looked back for a last stare at the rising moon. Providentially, at just that moment and at just that point where the reflection of the moon bobbed on the water, a beaver's head broke the surface. Gliding its way through the moonlight, the beaver saw me off.

I added my voice to earth's chorus: "Praise to the Lord, the Almighty, the King of creation."

Conclusion

On Wings like Eagles

The LORD is the everlasting God,
    the Creator of the ends of the earth.
He will not grow tired or weary,
    and his understanding no one can fathom.
He gives strength to the weary
    and increases the power of the weak.
Even youths grow tired and weary,
    and young men stumble and fall;
but those who hope in the LORD
    will renew their strength.
They will soar on wings like eagles;
    they will run and not grow weary;
    they will walk and not be faint.

Isaiah 40:28–31

The other day a fish flew over my house. I'm not kidding. It was about forty feet in the air, and it swam in a graceful curve over our house and into the woods behind. The fish was at least two feet long, and I could clearly see its tail flapping back and forth as it wended its way merrily through the wind currents.

One little detail I forgot to mention: it was clutched firmly—head first and right side up—in the talons of a red-tailed hawk, which was circling low over our rooftop, looking for a place to, um, perch.

Flying Fish

You and I were made to fly, not to swim.

We began this book with the image of time being like a river current. But common as the metaphor is in our culture, and apt as it is to our experience, Scripture never once speaks of human beings bobbing about in the river of time. In fact, in the pages of Scripture, we are compared to all manner of flying things, not swimming things: to swallows that dwell near God in the temple (Ps. 84:1–4), to chicks gathered under God's protective wing (Ps. 91:1–4), to doves vulnerable and innocent (Matt. 10:16), to sparrows watched over by the Father (Matt. 10:29), to ravens for whom our heavenly Father provides (Luke 12:24). And to eagles strengthened and upheld by God (Isa. 40:28–31).

God made us to soar—to soar on wings like eagles.

Easier said than done.

"Wally, the status report that you emailed me is blank."

In this *Dilbert* cartoon, Wally's boss has dropped by his cubicle. Wally turns to him, coffee cup in hand. "That's because eagles can't type."

"What?" his boss asks.

Wally explains: "The motivational poster in the break room says I should be like an eagle."

"The point of that poster," says his exasperated boss, "is that your spirit should soar like an eagle while you continue to do mundane work."

"Wouldn't I die," Wally asks, "if my spirit left my body to go soar?"

The boss tries to clarify: "You're confusing your spirit with your soul. While your spirit is soaring, your soul should remain trapped in your body slowly decaying while you create your status report."[1]

As I sat in the dim control room at the Indy airport, the air traffic controllers around me juggling the relentless flow of planes across their airspace, I found myself getting tired just watching them. Those little dots just kept coming and coming and coming.

At the end of my visit, I commented on how hard it must be to deal with the never-ending pressure. Scott leaned forward, raising his eyebrows as he does, and said it was only going to get worse. Not only are new flights being added to the skies every day, but carriers, desperate to save money, are pushing for ever-narrower safety margins. So urgent is the press for airlines to save money that the profits or losses of the major carriers now show up as one dimension of the performance reviews for air traffic controllers! He shook his head. I could see the strain in his eyes and hear it in his voice.

Trying to fit more and more flights into a finite amount of airspace. Why did that seem so familiar? And why did the stress feel so familiar too?

Living Well

In the end, a life well lived is not the outcome of some sort of calendar calculus. It isn't arrived at by just the right additions and subtractions to our daily schedule. Even the disciplines of rest—Sabbath, sleep, retreat—bring but a modicum of rest, and that short-lived. The tranquility, the soul rest, for which we long ultimately lies deeper than time, with the Author of time. Only as we yield our lives up to him and allow him to order our days will our lives take the shape they are meant to have, and we will enter into his rest. Tranquility comes on the other side of relinquishment, not accomplishment.

We are not called to fit an infinite number of things into a finite amount of time. Rather, God calls us to understand the times, to make the most of the time, and to trust him with the rest.

While we walk this earth, the clock will never cease to tick, scolding us with its relentless demands. But it is on the Lord's face, not on the face of the clock, that our eyes should ultimately rest. We wait for that day when, by his mercy, he will say to us not "Final performance review: punctuality 6.7, efficiency 7.2, productivity 5.8" but "Well done, good and faithful servant! . . . Come and share your master's happiness" (Matt. 25:21).

Circling

On a quiet, fragrant Monday after a particularly full Easter week, I headed south in my car along the Wabash River to a place I'd long wanted to explore: Black Rock. The sandstone cliffs, the highest point within a hundred miles, dominate the water where it bends south, making them a perfect outlook for Chief Tecumseh's scouts two hundred years before.

After exploring the promontory and the various caves about the rock face, I picked my way down through the poison ivy and thorns to the riverside, where I hopped onto a boulder that had toppled into the river ages before. There I sat in the morning sunshine. The spring current was surprisingly swift; from time to time the silvery tail of a fish broke the surface.

Movement to my left caught my eye. I turned just in time to see a huge bird flap along the river bend and out of sight, too quickly for me to pick it up with my binoculars but not too quickly for me to notice its distinctive white head and tail. A bald eagle!

With my binoculars, I watched the eagle for four or five minutes as it came back my way. It flew back and forth across the river, out over the bank on each side and then back over the river. Its wide wings flapped four or five times in a row, rested for a beat, flapped, rested, flapped, rested. With such massive wings—a seven-foot span—gaining altitude was difficult, so it remained low. Its seemingly aimless turns made me think it was fishing, and it was, but not for lunch.

Slowly the bird made its way downriver, coming closer and closer to where I sat. Through my binoculars I could see it looking about as it flew, its primary feathers—the "fingers" at the end of its wings—held together to reduce drag as it drummed the air, its tail drawn tight, angling now left, now right, as it wended its way.

Then, immediately above me, it veered sharply, fanning and pressing its tail to the right while banking its wings steeply to the left. It locked its wings flat, feathered its tail wide, spread its primaries to maximize lift, and—without another flap of its wings—circled in tight soaring spirals, rising higher and higher and higher. It had found what it was fishing for: a thermal, an invisible column of rising air above a warm patch of earth. The eagle simply spread its wings and rose, climbing as fast as ten miles per hour.

High overhead, it turned almost as abruptly out of the top of the thermal, tucked its wings into a delta, and shot westward on a swift descent, its streamlined form easily approaching sixty miles per hour, again without a flap of its wings.

Ornithologists refer to it as soaring migration. Isaiah calls it soaring on wings like eagles. Find a thermal, soar up inside of it, top out of it in a tuck, glide down to the base of the next one, soar up again, and so on. Spiral up, glide down. By gliding from thermal to thermal, eagles are able to fly three or four hundred miles without once flapping their wings.

This is living as God intends it to look.

Our primary job is to seek the invisible source of power, to seek where God is working, to circle and seek and search—to wait—until we come upon his uplifting presence, and then to do everything in our power to remain there, allowing him to raise us up on wings like eagles. Either we're in God's hands, or we're looking for them. Either way—rising or gliding—we are resting in him.

"'Not by might nor by power, but by my Spirit,' says the LORD Almighty" (Zech. 4:6).

In that—in him—is tranquility.

Overcome by the glorious in-breaking participation of God in every aspect of life, Annie Dillard whispers, "I live in tranquility and trembling."[2] Might we all.

With God let all things begin.
With God let all things rest.
Amish bookplate, 1845

Notes

Preface

1. Thomas à Kempis, *Come, Lord Jesus: Devotional Readings from "The Imitation of Christ,"* ed. David Hazard (Minneapolis: Bethany House, 1999), 151.

2. George Herbert, "The Thanksgiving," in *The Complete English Works*, ed. Ann Pasternak Slater (New York: Alfred A. Knopf, 1995), 32.

Chapter 1: Busy, Busy, Busy

1. Ralph Keyes, *Timelock: How Life Got So Hectic and What You Can Do about It* (New York: HarperCollins, 1991), 3.

2. Susan Brenna, "I'm Totally Stressed Out," *Seventeen*, February 1996, 123.

3. "Caught in a Vicious Cycle," *Sales and Marketing Management*, January 1997, 49–50.

4. Nancy Gibbs, "How America Has Run Out of Time," *Time*, April 24, 1989, 64.

5. Alfred, Lord Tennyson, "Dark Verge of Life," in *Poetry for the Soul*, ed. Mary Batchelor (Nashville: Moorings, 1995), 473.

6. "The OEC: Facts about the Language," Oxford Dictionaries website, accessed March 9, 2015, http://www.oxforddictionaries.com/us/words/the-oec-facts-about-the-language.

7. Bruce Eric Kaplan, *No One You Know* (New York: Simon & Schuster, 1999), 187.

8. Robert Mankoff, *New Yorker*, May 3, 1993, 50, http://observer.com/2003/05/how-about-never/#ixzz2lagfG1x7.

Chapter 2: The Busyness Factory

1. Lucy Bannerman, "Cambridge Reveals the Time-Eater, Chronophage, Devourer of Hours," *Times of London*, September 19, 2008, http://www.thetimes.co.uk/tto/news/uk/article1967075.ece.

2. Thorleif Boman, *Hebrew Thought Compared with Greek* (New York: W. W. Norton, 1970), 150.

3. Ibid.

4. Daniel J. Boorstin, *The Discoverers* (New York: Random House, 1983), 27.

5. Sara Schechner, "The Time of Day," in *The Discovery of Time*, ed. Stuart McCready (Naperville, IL: Sourcebooks, 2001), 125–26.

6. Ibid., 37.

7. Susan J. White, *Christian Worship and Technological Change* (Nashville: Abingdon, 1994), 67.

8. Ralph Keyes, *Timelock: How Life Got So Hectic and What You Can Do about It* (New York: HarperCollins, 1991), 20.

9. Ibid.

10. Ibid., 327.

11. Ibid., 39–40.

12. James Jespersen and Jane Fitz-Randolph, *From Sundials to Atomic Clocks: Understanding Time and Frequency*, 2nd rev. ed. (Mineola, NY: Dover Publications, 1999), 57–59.

13. Keyes, *Timelock*, 35.

14. Robert Levine, *A Geography of Time: The Temporal Misadventures of a Social Psychologist* (New York: Basic Books, 1997), 67.

15. Ibid., 70–72.

16. James Gleick, *Faster: The Acceleration of Just about Everything* (New York: Pantheon, 1999), 153.

17. Personal conversation with Dennis Widenaur, 2004.

18. Lecture notes from talk given at Wheaton College, October 2009.

Chapter 3: The Inner Hurricane

1. Robert M. Sapolsky, *Why Zebras Don't Get Ulcers: An Updated Guide to Stress, Stress-Related Diseases, and Coping* (New York: W. H. Freeman, 1994), 280–83.

2. Meyer Friedman and Ray Rosenman, *Type A Behavior and Your Heart* (New York: Alfred A. Knopf, 1974), 60.

3. Meyer Friedman and Diane Ulmer, *Treating Type A Behavior and Your Heart* (New York: Alfred A. Knopf, 1984), 56.

4. Friedman and Rosenman, *Type A Behavior and Your Heart*, 72.

5. Ralph Keyes, *Timelock: How Life Got So Hectic and What You Can Do about It* (New York: HarperCollins, 1991), 115.

6. Friedman and Rosenman, *Type A Behavior and Your Heart*, 4.

7. Robert Levine, *A Geography of Time: The Temporal Misadventures of a Social Psychologist* (New York: Basic Books, 1997), 21–22.

8. Kathleen Lavey, "The Need for Speed," *Lafayette Journal and Courier*, April 5, 2006, D1.

9. Sapolsky, *Why Zebras Don't Get Ulcers*, 277.

10. http://en.wikipedia.org/wiki/User:Thomasmwells/Fomo.

11. Dave Barry, "Prepare Your Fetus for Harvard Now," *Lafayette Journal and Courier*, October 31, 2004, E9.

12. United States Department of Labor, Bureau of Labor Statistics, http://www.bls.gov/tus/charts/leisure.htm.

13. Kaiser Family Foundation Study, http://kff.org/disparities-policy/press-release/daily-media-use-among-children-and-teens-up-dramatically-from-five-years-ago/.

14. John Eagan, "A Traveler toward the Dawn," in Brennan Manning, *Abba's Child: The Cry of the Heart for Intimate Belonging* (Colorado Springs: NavPress, 2002), 51.

Chapter 4: Toward a Solution

1. Ralph Keyes, *Timelock: How Life Got So Hectic and What You Can Do about It* (New York: HarperCollins, 1991), 20.

2. Faith Popcorn and Lys Marigold, *Clicking* (New York: HarperCollins, 1996), 209.

3. Annie Gowen, "'Lifestyle Managers' Run Errands, and Lives, for Families," *Lafayette Journal and Courier*, December 19, 2007, D3.

4. James Gleick, *Faster: The Acceleration of Just about Everything* (New York: Pantheon, 1999), 168.

5. Barbara Nachman, "Are You Eating While Reading This? Welcome to Multitasking," *Lafayette Journal and Courier*, October 1, 1998, D1.

6. Sandra Blakeslee, "Study: Brain Bad at Juggling Two Complex Tasks at Once," *Denver Post*, July 31, 2001, 1A.

7. Linda Stone, "Continuous Partial Attention," *Linda Stone* (blog), accessed November 24, 2013, http://lindastone.net/qa/continuous-partial-attention/.

8. William Shakespeare, *King Richard III*, act 4, scene 1 (London: J. M. Dent & Sons, 1935), 70.

9. Richard Baxter, *The Reformed Pastor* (Lafayette, IN: Sovereign Grace Publishers, 2000), 82.

10. Eliza to her sister Georgiana in Charlotte Brontë, *Jane Eyre* (London: Penguin, 2006), 271–72.

11. Thomas Blague, "A Sermon Preached at the Charterhouse, before the Kings Majestie," London, May 10, 1603, quoted in Daniel Swift, *Shakespeare's Common Prayers: The Book of Common Prayer and the Elizabethan Age* (Oxford: Oxford University Press, 2013), 166.

Chapter 5: Deep Time

1. R. C. Trench, *Trench's Synonyms of the New Testament* (Peabody, MA: Hendrickson, 2000), 221.

2. Hans-Christoph Hahn, "Time," in *Dictionary of New Testament Theology*, vol. 3, ed. Colin Brown (Grand Rapids: Zondervan, 1978), 834.

3. Ibid., 832.

4. T. S. Eliot, "The Dry Salvages," in *Collected Poems 1909–1962* (New York: Harcourt Brace and Company, 1963), 194.

5. Hahn, "Time," 843–84.

6. Trench, *Trench's Synonyms of the New Testament*, 222.

7. Victor Hugo, *Les Miserables*, trans. Norman Denny (New York: Penguin, 2012), 110–11.

Chapter 6: While There Is Time

1. Thomas Traherne, "Meditation 243," *Centuries of Meditation* (New York: Cosimo, 2007), 183–84.

2. My friend Jason McKnight pointed out that three of these redemptive eras end with the announcement "It is finished" (or the equivalent): at the end of creation (Gen. 2:2); at the end of Jesus's life and ministry (John 19:30); and at the end of the new creation (Rev. 21:6 NLT). Tellingly, the one era that is of our own making—misery—does not end with these words. We think we are finished by our sin, but, by the grace of God, we are not.

3. Thomas à Kempis, *The Imitation of Christ*, trans. E. M. Blaiklock (Nashville: Thomas Nelson, 1979), 158–59.

Chapter 7: The Circle and the Arrow

1. Sheldon Vanauken, *A Severe Mercy* (San Francisco: Harper & Row, 1977), 203.

2. Herman Bavinck, *The Doctrine of God*, trans. William Hendriksen (Grand Rapids: Baker, 1951), 156.

Chapter 8: The Vanishing Point

1. Amy Patterson-Neubert, "Taking One Day at a Time," *Journal and Courier*, May 12, 2002, E1.

2. Diane Ackerman, *Dawn Light: Dancing with Cranes and Other Ways to Start the Day* (New York: W. W. Norton, 2009), 178–79.

3. Jonathan Edwards, quoted in Steven J. Lawson, *The Unwavering Resolve of Jonathan Edwards* (Lake Mary, FL: Reformation Trust, 2008), 96.

Chapter 9: Whose Time Is It?

1. C. S. Lewis, *The Screwtape Letters; with Screwtape Proposes a Toast*, rev. ed. (New York: Collier, 1982), 96–97.

2. Eric Mataxas, *Amazing Grace* (New York: HarperCollins, 2007), 64.

3. Sandra Cronk, "Gelassenheit: The Rites of the Redemptive Process in Old Order Amish and Old Order Mennonite Communities," *Mennonite Quarterly Review* 55 (1981): 7–8, quoted in Donald Kraybill, Steven Nolt, and David L.

Weaver-Zercher, *Amish Grace: How Forgiveness Transcended Tragedy* (San Francisco: Jossey-Bass, 2007), 101.

4. Ibid., 115.

5. Ibid., 167.

6. Dietrich Bonhoeffer, *Life Together* (New York: Harper & Row, 1954), 99.

7. Gordon MacDonald, *Ordering Your Private World* (Nashville: Thomas Nelson, 1985), 33.

Chapter 10: A Single Eye

1. Jorge Luis Borges, "The Garden of Forking Paths," in *Labyrinths: Selected Stories and Other Writings*, ed. Donald A. Yates and James E. Irby (New York: New Directions), 20.

2. Dag Hammarskjöld, *Markings*, trans. Leif Sjöberg and W. H. Auden (New York: Alfred A. Knopf, 1964), 74.

3. Francis de Sales, cited in *The Wisdom of the Saints*, ed. Jill Haak Adels (New York: Oxford University Press, 1987), 30.

4. Bill Amend, *Fox Trot, Lafayette Journal and Courier*, September 12, 2006, D4.

5. Maggie Jackson, *Distracted: The Erosion of Attention and the Coming Dark Age* (Amherst, NY: Prometheus, 2008), 259.

6. Leighton Ford, *The Attentive Life: Discerning God's Presence in All Things* (Downers Grove, IL: InterVarsity, 2008), 43.

7. William James, *The Principles of Psychology*, cited in Jackson, *Distracted*, 260.

Chapter 11: Moments Burdened with Glorious Purpose

1. Augustine, *The Confessions*, book VIII, 5.12, trans. Maria Boulding (New York: Random House, 1997), 155.

2. Ibid., 165.

3. David H. Stern, "Commentary on Luke 10:4," in *The Jewish New Testament Commentary* (Clarksville, MD: Jewish New Testament Publications, 1999), 121.

Chapter 12: The One Thing

1. Rabbi Dimi of Nehardea, Babylonian Talmud, *Shabbath* 127a, contemporary paraphrase, http://halakhah.com/shabbath/shabbath_127.html.

2. Rabbi Eliezer, Babylonian Talmud, *Berakoth* 63b, contemporary paraphrase, http://halakhah.com/berakoth/berakoth_63.html.

3. Rabbi Hamnuna, Babylonian Talmud, *Berakoth* 58a, contemporary paraphrase, http://halakhah.com/berakoth/berakoth_58.html.

4. Evelyn Underhill, *Concerning the Inner Life with the House of the Soul* (Eugene, OR: Wipf & Stock, 1947), 99.

5. Charles H. Spurgeon, January 24, evening, *Morning and Evening*, in Joanna Weaver, *Having a Mary Heart in a Martha World: Finding Intimacy with God in the Busyness of Life* (Colorado Springs: WaterBrook, 2000), 62.

6. Ibid., 9.

7. Oswald Chambers, "October 19," *My Utmost for His Highest* (Westwood, NJ: Barbour and Company, 1963).

Chapter 14: Soul Rest

1. Minnie Louise Haskins, "God Knows," *Rotarian* 57, no. 4 (October 1940).

2. Erwin Goedicke, unpublished journal entry shared in personal correspondence, February 11, 2005. Used by permission.

Chapter 15: The Beautiful Life

1. Sebastian Junger, *The Perfect Storm* (New York: HarperCollins, 1997), 98–99, 177.

2. Gale Sayers, *I Am Third* (New York: Bantam Books, 1972), 43.

3. C. S. Lewis, *The Four Loves* (Orlando: Harcourt, 1960), 122–23.

4. Francis de Sales, *Introduction to the Devout Life* (New York: Doubleday, 1989), 95–96.

5. Jeremie Begbie, *Theology, Music and Time* (Cambridge, UK: Cambridge University Press, 2000), 49.

Chapter 16: Still Life

1. Paul Rezendes, *Tracking and the Art of Seeing* (Charlotte, VT: Camden House, 1992), 140–41.

2. Joel Chandler Harris, *Uncle Remus: His Songs and Sayings* (New York: Penguin, 1982), 62.

3. Kat Duff, *The Secret Life of Sleep* (New York: Simon & Schuster, 2014), 185.

4. Ibid., 186.

5. John Milton, *Paradise Lost*, ed. John Elledge (New York: W. W. Norton, 1975), 96.

6. Eugene Peterson, "The Pastor's Sabbath," *Leadership* (spring 1985), 53, quoted in Marva J. Dawn, *Keeping the Sabbath Wholly: Ceasing, Resting, Embracing, Feasting* (Grand Rapids: Eerdmans, 1989), 58.

7. "Night Prayer," *The New Zealand Prayer Book* (New York: HarperOne, 1997), 184.

8. The word ("work") used for what is prohibited in these verses is the same word used in 31:1–7 to describe the craftsmanship and construction skills necessary to build the tabernacle.

9. See *Mishnah Shabbat* and *Mishnah Erubin*, in *The Mishnah*, trans. Henry Danby (Oxford: Oxford University Press, 1987), 100–135.

10. Joy Davidman, *Smoke on the Mountain* (Philadelphia: Westminster, 1954), 59.

11. Ruth Haley Barton, spiritual formation lecture notes, Transforming Center, Chicago, IL, January 24, 2011.

12. Abraham Joshua Heschel, *The Sabbath* (New York: Farrar, Straus & Giroux, 1951), 29.

13. H. L. Mencken, *A Mencken Chrestomathy* (New York: Random House, 1982), 624.

14. Dawn, *Keeping the Sabbath Wholly*, 5.

Chapter 17: Deeper Still

1. Gordon MacDonald, *Restoring Your Spiritual Passion* (Nashville: Oliver Nelson, 1986), 26.

2. Amy Carmichael, "Moonlight," *Mountain Breezes: The Collected Poems of Amy Carmichael* (Fort Washington, PA: Christian Literature Crusade, 1999), 127.

3. Cornelius Plantinga Jr., "Background Noise," *Books and Culture*, July/August 1995, 8.

4. David Brooks, "Time to Do Everything except Think," *Newsweek*, April 30, 2001, 71.

5. Charles Spurgeon, "The Christian Minister's Private Prayer," *The Sword and the Trowel*, http://www.godrules.net/library/spurgeon/NEW9spurgeon_b11.htm.

6. Isaac Watts, "I Sing the Mighty Power of God," in *The Covenant Hymnal* (Chicago: Covenant Press, 1973), no. 80.

7. Annie Dillard, *Pilgrim at Tinker Creek* (New York: HarperCollins, 1998), 274.

8. Elizabeth Barrett Browning, "Aurora Leigh," in *The Treasury of Religious Verse*, ed. Donald T. Kauffman (Westwood, NJ: Fleming H. Revell, 1962), 11.

Conclusion

1. Scott Adams, *Dilbert, Journal and Courier*, June 5, 2005.

2. Annie Dillard, *Pilgrim at Tinker Creek* (New York: HarperCollins, 1998), 274.

Select Bibliography

What follows is a list of those works I've found most directly relevant to the themes I've touched on in this book. They cover a wide range of genres: fiction, history, philosophy, science, spirituality, societal commentary, practical advice. Not all are ones I agree with; nor are they all ones I would recommend. But each has a place on the list either because of the way it captures our culture's view of time or because of the way it has shaped my own.

Achelis, Elisabeth. *Of Time and the Calendar*. New York: Hermitage House, 1955.

Ackerman, Diane. *Dawn Light: Dancing with Cranes and Other Ways to Start the Day*. New York: W. W. Norton, 2009.

Anderson, Fil. *Running on Empty: Contemplative Spirituality for Overachievers*. Colorado Springs: WaterBrook, 2004.

Asimakoupoulos, Greg, John Maxwell, and Steve McKinley. *The Time Crunch: What to Do When You Can't Do It All*. Sisters, OR: Multnomah, 1993.

Banks, Robert. *Redeeming the Routines: Bringing Theology to Life*. Wheaton: BridgePoint, 1993.

————. *The Tyranny of Time: When Twenty-Four Hours Is Not Enough.* Eugene, OR: Wipf & Stock, 1983.

Barton, Ruth Haley. *Invitation to Solitude and Silence: Experiencing God's Transforming Presence.* Downers Grove, IL: InterVarsity, 2004.

Bass, Dorothy C. *Receiving the Day: Christian Practices for Opening the Gift of Time.* San Francisco: Jossey-Bass, 2000.

Begbie, Jeremy S. *Theology, Music and Time.* Cambridge, UK: Cambridge University Press, 2000.

Bevere, Lisa. *Out of Control and Loving It! Giving God Complete Control of Your Life.* Orlando: Creation House, 1996.

Boyd, Brady. *Addicted to Busy: Recovery for the Rushed Soul.* Colorado Springs: David C. Cook, 2014.

Brand, Stewart. *The Clock of the Long Now: Time and Responsibility.* New York: Basic Books, 1999.

Breedlove, Sally. *Choosing Rest: Cultivating a Sunday Heart in a Monday World.* Colorado Springs: NavPress, 2002.

Briscoe, Pete, and Patricia Hickman. *Secrets from the Treadmill: Discover God's Rest in the Busyness of Life.* Nashville: Nelson Books, 2004.

Buchanan, Mark. *The Rest of God: Restoring Your Soul by Restoring Sabbath.* Nashville: Thomas Nelson, 2006.

Burns, Lee. *Busy Bodies: Why Our Time-Obsessed Society Keeps Us Running in Place.* New York: W. W. Norton, 1993.

Chen, Pauline W. *Final Exam: A Surgeon's Reflections on Mortality.* New York: Vintage Books, 2008.

Chester, Tim. *The Busy Christian's Guide to Busyness.* Nottingham, UK: Inter-Varsity, 2006.

Craig, William Lane. *Time and Eternity: Exploring God's Relationship to Time.* Wheaton: Crossway, 2001.

Daily, Carrie J. *Families and Time: Keeping Pace in a Hurried Culture.* Thousand Oaks, CA: Sage Publications, 1996.

Dawn, Marva J. *Keeping the Sabbath Wholly: Ceasing, Resting, Embracing, Feasting.* Grand Rapids: Eerdmans, 1989.

de Caussade, Jean-Pierre. *The Sacrament of the Present Moment.* Translated by Kitty Muggeridge. San Francisco: HarperSanFrancisco, 1989.

De Graza, Sebastian. *Of Time, Work, and Leisure.* New York: Vintage, 1962.

Deweese, Garrett J. *God and the Nature of Time.* Bodmin, Cornwall, UK: Ashgate Publishing, 2004.

DeYoung, Kevin. *Crazy Busy: A (Mercifully) Short Book about a (Really) Big Problem*. Wheaton: Crossway, 2013.

Duff, Kat. *The Secret Life of Sleep*. New York: Simon & Schuster, 2014.

Easwaran, Eknath. *Take Your Time: Finding Balance in a Hurried World*. New York: Hyperion, 1994.

Edwards, Tilden. *Sabbath Time*. Nashville: Upper Room Publishers, 1992.

Emerson, Ralph Waldo, and Henry David Thoreau. *Nature and Walking*. Boston: Beacon, 1991.

Evans, Pamela. *The Over-Committed Christian: Serving God without Wearing Out*. Downers Grove, IL: InterVarsity, 2001.

Eyre, Linda, and Richard Eyre. *Lifebalance: How to Simplify and Bring Harmony to Your Everyday Life*. New York: Fireside, 1997.

Fading, Alan. *An Unhurried Life: Following Jesus' Rhythms of Work and Life*. Downers Grove, IL: InterVarsity, 2013.

Farrar, Steve, and Mary Farrar. *Overcoming Overload: Seven Ways to Find Rest in Your Chaotic World*. Sisters, OR: Multnomah, 2003.

Ferrell, Kate, ed. *Time's River: The Voyage of Life in Art and Poetry*. New York: Bullfinch Press, 1999.

Flaherty, Michael G. *A Watched Pot: How We Experience Time*. New York: New York University Press, 1999.

Ford, Leighton. *The Attentive Life: Discerning God's Presence in All Things*. Downers Grove, IL: InterVarsity, 2008.

Frazee, Randy. *Making Room for Life: Trading Chaotic Lifestyles for Connected Relationships*. Grand Rapids: Zondervan, 2003.

Gaede, S. D. *Life in the Slow Lane: The Benefits of Not Getting What You Want When You Want It*. Grand Rapids: Zondervan, 1991.

Ganssle, Gregory, ed. *God and Time: Four Views*. Downers Grove, IL: InterVarsity, 2001.

Gire, Ken. *The Reflective Life: Becoming More Spiritually Sensitive to the Everyday Moments of Life*. Colorado Springs: Chariot Victor, 1998.

Gleick, James. *Faster: The Acceleration of Just about Everything*. New York: Pantheon, 1999.

Grudin, Robert. *Time and the Art of Living*. New York: Harper & Row, 1982.

Hansel, Tim. *When I Relax I Feel Guilty*. Elgin, IL: David C. Cook, 1979.

Hawking, Stephen. *A Brief History of Time*. 10th anniversary ed. New York: Bantam, 1998.

Heschel, Abraham Joshua. *The Sabbath: Its Meaning for Modern Man*. New York: Farrar, Straus & Giroux, 2000.

Hobbs, Peter. *The Short Day Dying*. Orlando: Harcourt, 2005.

Hochschild, Arlie Russell. *The Time Bind: When Work Becomes Home and Home Becomes Work*. New York: Henry Holt, 1997.

Holford-Strevens, Leofranc. *The History of Time: A Very Short Introduction*. Oxford: Oxford University Press, 2005.

Honoré, Carl. *In Praise of Slowness: How a Worldwide Movement Is Challenging the Cult of Speed*. New York: HarperCollins, 2004.

Howard, J. Grant. *Balancing Life's Demands: A New Perspective on Priorities*. Sisters, OR: Multnomah, 1983.

Hoy, David Couzens. *The Time of Our Lives: A Critical History of Temporality*. Cambridge, MA: MIT Press, 2009.

Hummel, Charles. *Freedom from Tyranny of the Urgent*. Downers Grove, IL: InterVarsity, 1997.

Jackson, Maggie. *Distracted: The Erosion of Attention and the Coming Dark Age*. Amherst, NY: Prometheus, 2008.

Jensen, Mary. *Still Life: The Art of Nurturing a Tranquil Soul*. Sisters, OR: Multnomah, 1997.

Jespersen, James, and Jane Fitz-Randolph. *From Sundials to Atomic Clocks: Understanding Time and Frequency*. 2nd rev. ed. Mineola, NY: Dover Publications, 1999.

Johnson, Steven. *How We Got to Now: Six Innovations That Made the Modern World*. New York: Penguin, 2014.

Keyes, Ralph. *Timelock: How Life Got So Hectic and What You Can Do about It*. New York: HarperCollins, 1991.

Kimmel, Tim. *Little House on the Freeway: Help for the Hurried Home*. Sisters, OR: Multnomah, 1987.

Klein, Étienne. *Chronos: How Time Shapes Our Universe*. Translated by Glenn Burney. New York: Thunder's Mouth Press, 2005.

Klein, Stefan. *The Secret Pulse of Time: Making Sense of Life's Scarcest Commodity*. Translated by Shelly Frisch. Cambridge, MA: Da Capo Press, 2006.

Koyama, Kosuke. *Three Mile an Hour God: Biblical Reflections*. Maryknoll, NY: Orbis, 1979.

Kraybill, Donald. *The Riddle of Amish Culture*. Baltimore: Johns Hopkins University Press, 1989.

Landes, David S. *Revolution in Time: Clocks and the Making of the Modern World*. Rev. ed. Cambridge, MA: Harvard University Press, 2000.

Levine, Robert. *A Geography of Time: The Temporal Misadventures of a Social Psychologist*. New York: Basic Books, 1997.

Lindbergh, Anne Morrow. *A Gift from the Sea*. New York: Pantheon, 1955.

MacDonald, Gordon. *Ordering Your Private World*. Nashville: Oliver Nelson, 1984.

McCready, Stuart, ed. *The Discovery of Time*. Naperville, IL: Sourcebooks, 2001.

McCrossen, Alexis. *Holy Day, Holiday: The American Sunday*. Ithaca, NY: Cornell University Press, 2000.

Mikics, David. *Slow Reading in a Hurried Age*. Cambridge, MA: Belknap Press, 2013.

Montross, Christine. *Body of Work: Meditations on Mortality from the Human Anatomy Lab*. New York: Penguin, 2008.

Moore-Ede, Martin. *The Twenty-Four-Hour Society: Understanding Human Limits in a World That Never Stops*. Reading, MA: Addison-Wesley, 1993.

Neuhaus, Richard John. *As I Lay Dying: Meditations upon Returning*. New York: Basic Books, 2002.

Norris, Kathleen. *The Quotidian Mysteries: Laundry, Liturgy, and "Women's Work."* New York: Paulist Press, 1998.

Pepper, Elizabeth, and John Wilcock, eds. *A Book of Days: Wisdom through the Seasons*. Santa Barbara, CA: Capra Press, 1996.

Pieper, Josef. *Leisure: The Basis of Culture*. New York: Random House, 1963.

Postema, Don. *Space for God: Study and Practice of Spirituality and Prayer*. Grand Rapids: CRC Publications, 1983.

Robertson, Brian. *There's No Place like Work: How Business, Government, and Our Obsession with Work Have Driven Parents from Home*. Dallas: Spence Publishing, 2000.

Robinson, John P., and Geoffrey Godbey. *Time for Life: The Surprising Ways Americans Use Their Time*. 2nd ed. University Park: Pennsylvania State University Press, 1997.

Runcorn, David. *A Center of Quiet: Hearing God When Life Is Noisy*. Downers Grove, IL: InterVarsity, 1990.

Rybczynski, Witold. *Waiting for the Weekend*. New York: Penguin, 1991.

Ryken, Leland. *Redeeming the Time: A Christian Approach to Work and Leisure*. Grand Rapids: Baker, 1995.

Sapolsky, Robert M. *Why Zebras Don't Get Ulcers: An Updated Guide to Stress, Stress-Related Diseases, and Coping*. New York: W. H. Freeman, 1994.

Schor, Juliet. *The Overworked American: The Unexpected Decline of Leisure*. New York: HarperCollins, 1992.

Schulte, Brigid. *Overwhelmed: Work, Love, and Play When No One Has the Time*. New York: Farrar, Straus & Giroux, 2014.

Spark, Muriel. *Memento Mori*. New York: New Directions Books, 1959.

Stark, Peter. *Last Breath: Cautionary Tales from the Limits of Human Endurance*. New York: Ballantine, 2001.

Stevenson, Robert Louis. *An Apology for Idlers*. London: Penguin, 2009.

Swenson, Richard A. *Margin: Restoring Emotional, Physical, Financial, and Time Reserves to Overloaded Lives*. Colorado Springs: NavPress, 1992.

———. *The Overload Syndrome: Learning to Live within Your Limits*. Colorado Springs: NavPress, 1998.

Swenson, Richard A., and Karen Lee-Thorp. *Restoring Margin to Overloaded Lives*. Colorado Springs: NavPress, 1999.

Thurber, James. *The Thirteen Clocks*. New York: The New York Review of Books, 1950.

Tolstoy, Leo. *The Death of Ivan Ilyich*. Translated by Lynn Solotaroff. New York: Bantam, 1981.

Waugh, Alexander. *Time: Its Origins, Its Enigma, Its History*. New York: Carroll and Graf, 1999.

Weaver, Joanna. *Having a Mary Heart in a Martha World: Finding Intimacy with God in the Busyness of Life*. Colorado Springs: WaterBrook, 2002.

ALSO BY
DAVID W. HENDERSON